TARGETING
TURNOVER

Make Managers Accountable,
Win the Workforce Crisis

Richard P. Finnegan

BK

Berrett–Koehler Publishers, Inc.

Berrett-Koehler Publishers, Inc.
1333 Broadway, Suite P100
Oakland, CA 94612-1921
Tel: (510) 817-2277
Fax: (510) 817-2278
bkconnection.com

ORDERING INFORMATION
Quantity sales. Special discounts are available on quantity purchases by corporations, associations, and others. For details, please go to bkconnection.com to see our bulk discounts or contact bookorders@bkpub.com for more information.
Individual sales. Berrett-Koehler publications are available through most bookstores. They can also be ordered directly from Berrett-Koehler: Tel: (800) 929-2929; Fax: (802) 864-7626; bkconnection.com.
Orders for college textbook / course adoption use. Please contact Berrett-Koehler: Tel: (800) 929-2929; Fax: (802) 864-7626.

Distributed to the US trade and internationally by Penguin Random House Publisher Services.

The authorized representative in the EU for product safety and compliance is EU Compliance Partner, Pärnu mnt. 139b-14, 11317 Tallinn, Estonia, www.eucompliancepartner.com, +372 5368 65 02.

Berrett-Koehler and the BK logo are registered trademarks of Berrett-Koehler Publishers, Inc.

Printed in The United States of America

Berrett-Koehler books are printed on long-lasting acid-free paper. When it is available, we choose paper that has been manufactured by environmentally responsible processes. These may include using trees grown in sustainable forests, incorporating recycled paper, minimizing chlorine in bleaching, or recycling the energy produced at the paper mill.

Cataloging-in-Publication Data is on file at the Library of Congress.
Library of Congress Control Number: 2025003632
ISBN 9798890570840 (paperback) | ISBN 9798890570857 (pdf) | ISBN 9798890570864 (epub)

First Edition

33 32 31 30 29 28 27 26 25   10 9 8 7 6 5 4 3 2 1

Book production: Westchester Publishing Services
Cover design: Ashley Ingram

All case studies and company logos are printed with permission of those companies' executives. Finnegan's Arrow® copyright C-Suite Analytics and Richard P. Finnegan 2022. All rights reserved.

Author photo©Linda Wilson.

To my best friend, Lisa, who is also my wife.
Thanks for sharing your life with me.

Additional Books by Richard P. Finnegan

Rethinking Retention in Good Times and Bad
(Nicholas Brealey Publishing, ISBN: 978-1-47364-409-0)

The Power of Stay Interviews
(Society for Human Resource Management,
ISBN: 978-1-58644-234-7) (2012 ed.)

The Stay Interview
(AMACOM, ISBN: 978-0-81443-649-3)

Raise Your Team's Employee Engagement Score
(AMACOM, ISBN: 978-0-81443-862-6)

HR's Greatest Challenge
(Society for Human Resource Management,
ISBN: 978-1-58644-379-5)

Contents

Introduction

"An Ounce of Prevention Is Worth a Pound of Cure"

Benjamin Franklin gifted us with this quote nearly three hundred years ago when describing the importance of fire safety, although modern applications of it are more often about one's health. Nowhere does the literature confirm if Ben used this same phrase for preventing employee turnover, but I'd bet he would double down on applying this adage today. And if Ben had time traveled, what might he have written about quiet quitting, working from home, "work your wage," and the ongoing dispute about how many immigrants are too many? But then, nearly everyone was an immigrant back in Ben's time.

Saying employee retention has never mattered more in the United States is an easy argument. "Help wanted" signs abound due to the intersection of five factors: (1) our continuously humming, world-leading economy that requires a constant infusion of talent, (2) our fifty-year-plus birthrate drought, (3) an uncountable number of former corporate employees who are now entrepreneurs, (4) workers caught in a post-pandemic yawn about working at all, and (5) baby boomers like me who are exiting the workforce. Data and charts could highlight the impact of these factors, but what is more apparent is the worsening customer service caused by too few workers or workers who don't care enough.

This book presents a first-of-its-kind employee retention solution that is based on academic research versus what is commonly referred to as "best practices." *This research's most relevant finding is that the number one reason employees stay or leave is how much they trust their immediate, first-line supervisors.* This means each manager's individual relationship with each member of their team supersedes pay, benefits, recognition programs, onboarding, and all other one-size-fits-all programs that supposedly fix employee turnover. The latter are those generated from employee engagement surveys, exit interviews, employee focus groups, and other ways of trying to find "the thing" that will cause our good workers to stay. That "thing," I argue, is their supervisors, and it's been right under our collective noses all along.

This solution will direct us to manage employee retention as an *executive-driven business priority* rather than assigning HR to solve turnover, which is a certain step toward failure. And as a "recovering HR director," I say this with unwavering respect for my former colleagues who have been historically trapped between accountability for retention and having no responsibility for addressing those managers who drive good workers out the door.

Our solution is battle tested: you will read below about its application across eighteen Covenant Health facilities, twenty-two Wayne-Sanderson chicken-processing complexes, and sixty Clayton Homes factories, where turnover has been reduced by as much as 58 percent across the board. That solution includes costing, goal setting, forecasting, and accountability—the familiar methods and metrics companies have used for decades to improve sales, service, and ultimately profitability. Stay Interviews have been added to this mix, a concept I invented with a top-selling book in 2012, and which enables first-line leaders to learn the specific actions they should take to retain each individual employee.

If an ounce of prevention is indeed worth a pound of cure, this hints at a high ROI—16:1—on any prevention you put in place. You will leave this book fully grasping the financial waste resulting from all unwanted turnover and especially new-hire turnover. This doom-loop of hiring/training/replacing workers with new ones causes more errors, more injuries, and more customer turnoffs—all while preventing companies from adding to their headcounts to become more profitable.

Come join me in the pursuit of my own professional passion, to develop employee retention solutions that are based on solid research and that actually work. Accountants, purchasing agents, and all other professionals have begun their jobs for decades by knowing precisely what to do—having been handed predeveloped professional processes to guide them—yet providing executives with proven processes to retain their best workers has somehow fallen through the cracks.

Ben Franklin also taught us that "a penny saved is two pence clear." Let's now move forward together by retaining the workers we want, firing the ones we don't, and earning more than just a few additional pennies for our shareholders and our employees.

PART ONE

PROBLEM + SOLUTION

This section begins with data from the US Census Bureau that makes clear the alarming challenge we face finding qualified workers today and how much this challenge will increase in the future. Then follows an innovative, fresh-thinking solution for retaining your best employees that is based on solid research versus today's common and erroneous thinking on what supposedly makes employees stay. Also included are the exaggerated role of pay in retention, the best ideas for hiring employees who stay, and how to best leverage employee survey data.

1 ■ The Next Twenty Years

Beware the Pig in the Python

Any smart discussion about employee retention must begin by detailing the exceptionally steep hill we must climb to find and retain good workers in the immediate future and beyond. The next two decades will bring profound changes to the US workforce because our baby boomers are leaving us, resulting in insufficient increases of our worker numbers along with skepticism that new worker quality will be as good. China, Germany, Japan, South Korea, Canada, and other leading economies face the same stiff challenges, resulting in all high-income nations racing to import the best immigrants in order to sustain their economies.

But let's first look back on the people management challenges of the past twenty years, so we can compare the level of those obstacles to the ones contained in our twenty-years-out forecast.

Naming the COVID-19 pandemic as the major challenge of the past two decades is an easy call. A distant second would be the Great Recession. One way to compare the impact of each is to study the levels of workforce turbulence reported by the US Bureau of Labor Statistics.

Figure 1 compares key workforce data from the Great Recession's actual recession period of December 2007 to June 2009 to the same data points during the most crucial COVID-19 period of 2020 to 2022.[1]

The three data points of the "COVID-19 Era" column show the whiplash impact of initial workforce desperation, which was later followed by unprecedented workforce security ("COVID-19 Era" refers to March 2020–May 2023). The data show how our unemployment rate plummeted from nearly 15 percent down to 3.5 percent, all while open jobs increased nearly threefold; the Great Recession period never resulted in such extremes.

The pandemic era drove executive teams to invent health and safety solutions on the fly. The pandemic led to vaccination controversies; some workers being deemed "essential," which caused them to take maximum risks with their health; the overnight spike of employees working from home; working parents tending to homebound school children; and the coldness of quick business shutdowns that oftentimes sent people home for good with no severance.

Yet the United States recovered from the pandemic more quickly than other countries, such that many companies couldn't hire employees fast enough. Many of us still remember rushing to reopened restaurants only to then wait for tables because seating sections were closed due to staff shortages. This began the period that became known as the "Great Resignation."

These complex changes resulted in both good and bad impacts for the US workforce that will carry over into the next twenty years, as will the economic impact of our federal government's $5 billion bailout to households, mom-and-pop shops, local governments, schools, and other institutions.[2]

Economically, COVID-19 hit like an earthquake, suddenly and deeply, and was followed by fast infrastructure reconstruction. Our people-management assignment was to preserve the security of our workforce while matching them to jobs as the number of open jobs changed.

	COVID-19 Era	Great Recession
Lowest/highest unemployment rate	3.5% − 14.8%	4.9% − 9.5%
Lowest/highest monthly layoffs & discharges rate	.07% − 8.5%	1.1% − 2.5%
Lowest/highest monthly job openings	4.6 million − 12.2 million	2.2 million − 4.6 million

Figure 1: How Disruptive Was COVID-19 versus the Great Recession?
Source: US Census Bureau published data.

But the next twenty years will offer a far more profound, continual, and unavoidable challenge because the actual number of available workers will shrink relative to the number of jobs we will try to fill. And each of our fellow industrialized nations will be sitting in the same sinking boat.

Introducing the Great Gully

During the past year, I've collaborated with the US Census Bureau to learn the measurable impact of massive baby-boomer retirements coupled with our continuing low birthrate. We focused on the number of future Americans in the age group of eighteen to sixty-four, those of working age. Figure 2 depicts what I've named the "Great Gully" and compares the percentages of new additions to this group, looking backward and forward by presenting the data for the most recent twenty years and predicting the percentages for the next twenty years.[3]

Note that the chart does not predict that the number of working-age Americans will actually decrease by 2045—that will come later. Instead, the chart shows that future increases will be small fractions of the increases seen in the past. All of which invites the following question: Can the United States maintain its global economic dominance in the next twenty years and beyond while our number of working-age citizens remains relatively flat?

The Great Gully's projections are based in part on the chart in Figure 3.

Figure 3 shows US birthrates over the most recent eighty-plus year period, with each year measured against the "replacement level" of

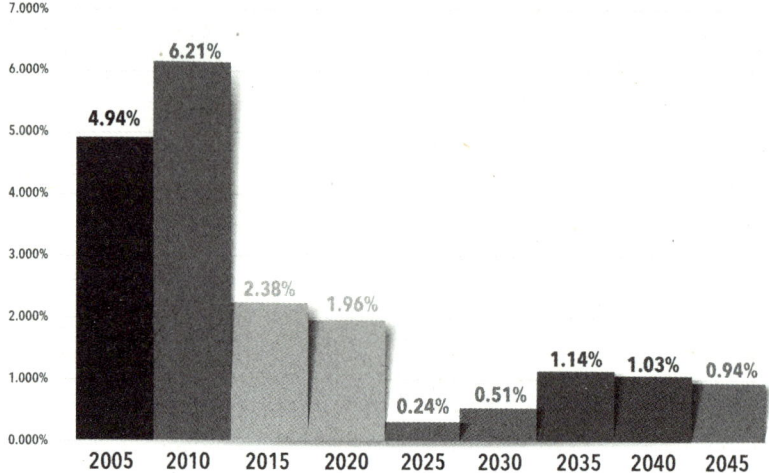

Figure 2: The Great Gully: US Five-Year Growth for the Working-Age Population versus US Annual Growth
Source: US Census Bureau published data.

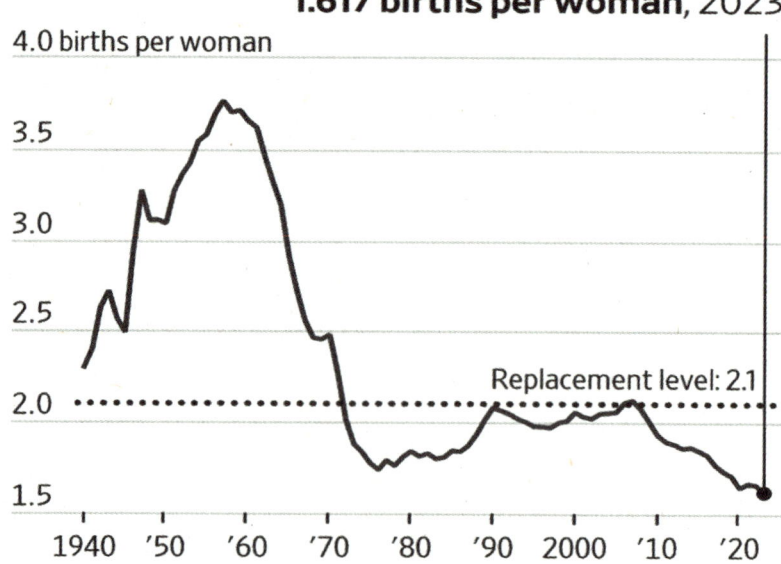

Figure 3: US Total Fertility Rate
Source: The Wall Street Journal. Used with permission of Dow Jones & Company, Inc., from *The Wall Street Journal*, Eastern Edition, April 25, 2025; permission conveyed through Copyright Clearance Center, Inc.

2.1. The replacement level indicates that each woman would have to give birth to an average of 2.1 babies during their lifetimes for our population to remain even.

The chart tells two different stories: before and after 1972. In the years before 1972, we see the following:

- The data reaches a high point in the early 1950s, when the United States settled into post–World War II normal living, when partners found each other and committed to raising traditional American families after delays imposed by the war.
- Marriages were more stable then and couples routinely had three or four children, unlike today.
- Most interesting to me is the vast gap between the number of babies born per woman during the World War II years of 1941–1945 as compared to the present time. Women were giving birth to about two times the number of children that are born today—and were doing so while the country was at war.

One wonders how this can possibly be true, yet it further underscores the relative scarcity of babies being born today. The Census Bureau in fact predicts that, for the first time in our history, older adults will outnumber children by 2034.[4]

This high-spiked period spawned a baby boom, and those born during the span of 1946 to 1964 became known as "baby boomers." As I write, our oldest baby boomers are seventy-nine and our youngest are sixty-one. Over thirty million Americans will reach the typical retirement age between 2024 and 2030, representing nearly 20 percent of our total workforce who are eligible to exit. That's a devastating number of likely workforce exits.[5]

After 1972, almost all of the years are below the replacement rate, culminating in the lowest-ever birthrate in 2023. Studies indicate that the rate couples are having kids has greatly slowed because of more women in the workplace, fewer people getting married, and the high cost of parenting, with one study declaring the main reason couples aren't having kids is "not wanting them."[6]

Given that 2023 was the year the United States experienced its lowest-ever birthrate to date and that the birthrate has been in free fall since 2008, there is no cause for optimism here. And recent reports indicate that our marriage rate is also declining, while just 14 percent of single Americans say they are looking for a partner.[7] And Americans across all ages are having less sex.[8]

If we are waiting for a revival spike of more American births, the cavalry isn't coming. *Instead, the Census Bureau predicts the continuing impact of low birth rates will push our total population to actually decline by the end of this century.*[9] The population peak year will be 2080 and then it's downhill from there. How will that impact the United States' global economic position and power?

COVID-19 Further Reduced the Workforce

This demographic pattern of baby boomers leaving the workforce and there not being enough kids produced to replace them has long been a slow-burning, pig-in-the-python fuse. Demographers decades ago predicted a future worker shortage, and that time is now. What could not have been predicted is that the pandemic took even more workers away, making a bad situation much worse.

In 2022, Federal Reserve chairman Jerome Powell announced there were 3.5 million fewer people in our workforce compared to pre-pandemic times.[10] He attributed most of these reductions to unplanned retirements as about two million older Americans unexpectedly walked away from their jobs shortly after the pandemic hit. COVID-19 deaths have also contributed as nearly 275,000 of COVID-19 deaths have involved Americans in our working-age group of eighteen to sixty-four.[11]

When I asked my Census Bureau contact if their projections accounted for these unexpected COVID-19-era losses, he replied, "Some, but not all." So the decreasing workforce data presented in the Great Gully chart (Figure 2) might actually be worse.

But perhaps the greatest drain on our numbers of workers from the pandemic has been the volume of former employees who have now cast themselves as entrepreneurs. Many of these are self-starting, long-hour workers who continue to contribute to our society but have separated themselves from the corporate world—and therefore from ever having bosses. Note how their historic growth mirrors the down-and-up impact of the pandemic.[12]

The data in Figure 4 represent only those who started businesses that require or benefit from paying for a government business license and who intend to hire workers. They omit, for example, our four-million-plus Uber and Lyft drivers, dog-sitters, and other gig economy workers who now disregard online job postings because they have sworn off big-business or so-called establishment jobs. And there is little reason to believe gig workers will return to establishment jobs as those companies will be outsourcing more work to gig workers because they won't find employees to put on their payrolls to do that work.

Put yourself in the place of a restaurant server in 2020. When the pandemic hit, you were instantaneously "furloughed" in March with likely no pay and then invited back when restaurants reopened a year later. Government money kept you partially afloat but landscaping work, delivering food, or dog-sitting contributed to needed cash flow. Or maybe you took online courses to chase an interest or prepare

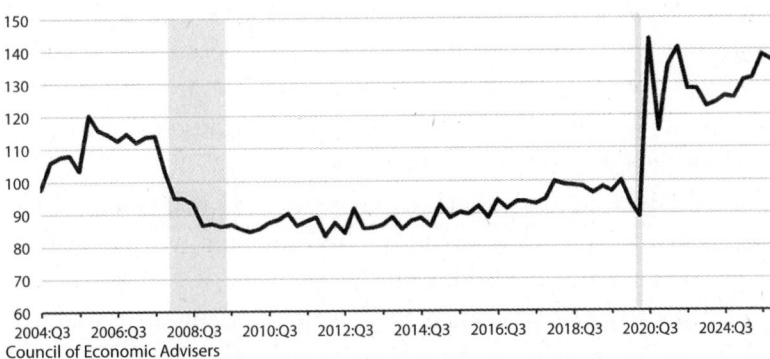

Council of Economic Advisers

Figure 4: US Total Monthly Business Applications for Likely Employers
Sources: US Census Bureau and Council of Economic Advisors calculations. Permission to reproduce.
Note: Number of applications is indexed to 2019 Q4. Employment-generating business applications are high-propensity business applications (HBA) as defined in the Census Business Formation Statistics. Gray bars indicate recessions.

for a better job. When your restaurant called a year later, you refused to return to a job that required working holidays, cleaning floors after midnight, and other aspects of restaurant-server jobs that most of us take for granted. In that interim period, you had become an entrepreneur who didn't require a business license.

This is why we had to stand in line waiting for tables after restaurants reopened. Those former servers had found better lives.

I recall reading about a mid-forties healthcare executive who said his greatest COVID-19-era joy while working from home was taking his two daughters to soccer practice. He subsequently quit his executive hospital job and became a self-employed consultant. He will still show up in federal workforce data as employed, but he is no longer available to any hospital or healthcare organization as a full-time employee.

COVID-19's Impact on Worker Preferences, Attitudes, and Grit

This same era gave birth to "quiet quitting," "work your wage," and other commitment-reducing terms, as well as pushed employees' interests forward regarding working from home and four-day work weeks. About 40 percent of our jobs can be done from home, which equates to sixty-seven million of them, and CEOs have vacillated on their return-to-office requirements lest they face the risk of added turnover. Twenty years ago, CEOs would say, "Jump!" and employees would say, "How high?" but not so today because the scarcity of workers gives them the power to swing decisions.

Certainly related is Gallup's reporting in 2024 that employee engagement was at an eleven-year low, and the drop was particularly acute among remote, hybrid, and younger workers.[13] Added to this are reports that young workers don't want the additional responsibilities that come with promotions, and that excessive numbers are ghosting job interviews as well as their first days of work.[14]

Much has been written about young workers' mental health since the pandemic, with the American Psychiatric Association reporting in 2023 that over half of young professional workers said they needed mental health help in the past year.[15] Reasons cited were the enormous growth of social media, political and cultural divisiveness, and unprecedented upheaval and change related to the pandemic. In addition, record numbers of young adults are living with their parents, bringing into question if this will further erode our workers' social and take-on-responsibility skills. [16]

The pandemic also left a negative trail with our children. Having missed out on traditional schooling, test scores are substantially down, absenteeism has nearly doubled, and homeschooling has seen an unprecedented surge.[17]

Gluing together young Americans' trends like more mental health issues, more adults living with parents, more absenteeism, less employee engagement, and less interest in relationships calls into question whether excessive social media has pushed our youth to be more distant and generally less involved, both in their work and in the lives of others.[18]

The baby-boomer generation they are replacing has been known for its workplace grit: arriving daily and on time, remaining until the work was done, and staying longer with each employer. COVID-19 created a massive interruption in young people's lives, and our nation looks forward to them thriving beyond all of the related setbacks as they move forward. With fingers crossed.

Middle-Age Wanderlust

Making things even worse, baby boomers are taking with them their just-a-few-jobs-for-life histories, which predicts worse employee retention for the future. Figure 5 makes clear that younger generations are staying with employers for far shorter periods of time than the older ones did.[19]

For reference:

- Gen Xers were born during the period of 1965 to 1980.
- Millennials were born during the period of 1981 to 1996.
- Gen Zers were born during the period of 1997 to 2012.

Many apply the term "millennials" to young people in general, yet, in reality, those millennials are now middle-aged or close to it.

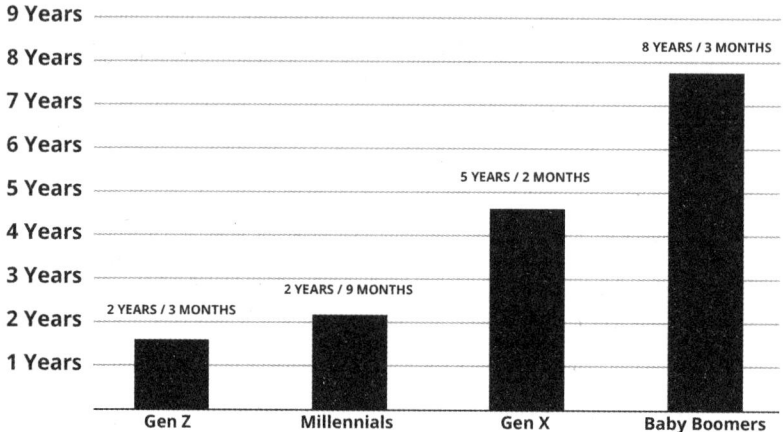

Figure 5: Average Length of Employment by Generation
Source: CareerBuilder published data.

Some of us have wondered if millennials could maintain their short job stints as they grew older while taking on families and other financial responsibilities. But the workforce shortage will further accommodate them in changing their day jobs while working their gig jobs by night. So, as baby boomers eventually move completely off the above chart, the time in the same job for the remaining generations will likely become even shorter.

Companies Are Already Desperate for Talent

It's become common to complain about poor customer service and to hear the "things aren't like they used to be" mutterings of those with clear memories of right-in-front-of-me employees who were always eager to help. And those who mutter are right because a full 75 percent of American businesses have already turned away customers or cut operating hours because they can't hire enough staff, making us wonder how much worse can customer service become.[20] Here are just a few examples that cut across many industries:

- Airlines are closing off routes due to pilot shortages while national safety experts are monitoring whether airlines are promoting junior pilots to bigger planes too quickly.[21]

- CVS, Walgreens, and Walmart have all reduced their pharmacy hours in the midst of a pharmacist shortage, and this is happening while public opinion of brick-and-mortar pharmacies is sinking fast.[22]
- A new hospital in Phoenix stood empty for six months because administrators couldn't find enough staff to provide services to patients.[23]
- School bus-driver shortages are forcing parents to drive their children to school, brought on by more flexible driving opportunities with Amazon, Uber, and other employers.[24]
- Parents also struggle to find childcare as 150,000 childcare workers have moved on to other jobs since before the pandemic.[25]
- Private and public sector employers are scaling back on college requirements, focusing instead on actual skills required for their jobs—and reducing the value of a college degree.[26]

On the legislative side, at least eleven states have sought to loosen their child labor laws. Iowa, for example, wishes to allow children as young as fourteen to work in meat coolers and industrial laundries, whereas lawmakers in Wisconsin believe those same fourteen-year-olds should be able to double as cocktail waitresses at night.[27]

On the military side, the US Army is offering up to $50,000 in hiring bonuses for qualified civilians, while the US Air Force has modified its fitness requirements by raising the acceptable levels of body fat.[28] The US Air Force just got fatter in order to better find and retain recruits.[29]

In my own county north of Orlando, officials are urging us to drive our own recyclables to the dump because they can't find and retain enough garbage truck drivers.[30] And our sheriff just lowered the age for jail detention officers from twenty-one to eighteen to fill open jobs.[31] The convicts they are guarding will benefit from our worker shortage too, as businesses are opening their doors to ex-cons, saying more than 80 percent of them are performing their jobs the same or better than other workers.[32]

Is Technology a Fix?

Remember when we feared that robots would take away all of our jobs, plunging America into high unemployment? Now we can't get enough of them to help keep our businesses afloat. Here are just a few of the bot inventions that are reducing the need for real people:

- Self-check-out technology in grocery stores, pharmacies, etc.
- Continuously improved ATMs to reduce bank staff and ultimately replace branches
- Automated ordering in restaurants to replace wait staff
- Purchasing online, which removes the sales rep
- Robo-calling telemarketers, whether we like them or not
- Robots that gather products in distribution centers, build cars, assist with surgeries, and more
- Self-driving cars and trucks, including commercial vehicles

And Avis, my Jamaican-born dry cleaner rep, has been replaced by a smooth-talking British-sounding female robot who instructs me on how to get my clothes cleaned, 24/7.

Of course, these robots require workers to design and develop them, which brings to mind this assessment from the Brookings Institution regarding AI's impact on job addition and subtraction:

> On one hand, automation often creates as many jobs as it destroys over time. Workers who can work with machines are more productive than those without them; this reduces both the costs and prices of goods and services, and makes consumers feel richer. As a result, consumers spend more, which leads to the creation of new jobs.[33]

The Inevitable and Unpopular Immigration Solution

Let's glue together these two very conflicting data sets. The US Census Bureau tells us that, beginning in 2030, 51 percent of our new working-age entrants will be immigrants, having been born outside of the United States, and this immigrant percentage will increase each year for as far as the Census Bureau projects. Here's their specific language: "Beginning in 2030 . . . immigration is projected to overtake natural increase (the excess of births over deaths) as the primary driver of population growth for the country." They go on to describe the 2030s as a "transformative decade for the U.S. population."[34] Yet US citizens' emotions about immigrants are not so welcoming, as Gallup's most recent polling says 55 percent of Americans want less immigration, while just 16 percent want more.[35]

Americans' opinions on immigration come as no surprise, perhaps based on media coverage of our Mexican border. The Carnegie Corporation has dug in on common perceptions about immigrants by providing facts versus commonly held perceptions. Here are a few of those misperceptions:

Myth #1: "Immigrants will take American jobs, lower wages, and especially hurt the poor."

Myth #2: "It is easy to immigrate here legally. Why don't illegal immigrants just get in line?"

Myth #3: "Immigrants abuse the welfare state."

Myth #4: "Immigrants are a major source of crime."

Myth #5: "Immigrants pose a unique risk today because of terrorism."[36]

Few Americans would guess the disproportionate roles immigrants played in our surviving COVID-19: the US pharmaceutical companies that developed vaccines were founded by immigrants, and a disproportionate number of all US healthcare workers were born outside of our country.[37]

Record numbers of immigrants have entered our labor force since the pandemic, and, more importantly, 68 percent of them are working or seeking work, compared to just 62 percent of native-born Americans.[38]

The Global Workforce Population Conundrum

As noted earlier, the US population will begin to decrease in 2080, while the amount of working-age Americans will decrease before then.[39] This might cause economists to predict doom for the US homebound economy—except for the fact that all our high-income industrial competitors are heading in the same direction.

Country-specific data is astounding. The German working population will reduce by a third by the end of this century; Italy, Spain, and Greece will lose half of their total workforces; and Poland, Portugal, Romania, Japan, and China will all lose up to two-thirds of their labor force.[40] Another report details that by as soon as 2030 the world will be short by eighty-five million workers, the approximate population of Germany. Six million of these shortages will be in the United States.[41]

Sampling national responses, Germany has legislated an immigration skill-based point system, South Korea is considering paying a $70,000 bonus for each newborn child, while Japan has rejected immigration as a fix and is instead implementing "womenomics," asking more of their women to join their workforce.[42]

Russia's baby-shortage solution is quite different, where the minister of health for the region of Primorsky Krai instructed that having a busy career wasn't an excuse for not having a family, and that people could choose to "create offspring" during work breaks.[43] There was no mention of wine or candles.

South Korea's birthrate has fallen to the world's lowest, resulting in sales of dog strollers outselling sales of baby strollers. The then president declared this to be a national emergency, all while he and his wife had no children but ten cats and dogs.[44]

The driver again is low birthrates, and global birthrates vary greatly among nations and income levels. These data on 2022 birthrates come via the World Bank.[45]

Selected birthrates by region:

- Arab world: 3.1
- Australia: 1.6
- East Asia and the Pacific: 1.5
- European area: 1.4
- Latin America and the Caribbean: 1.8
- North America: 1.6
- Sub-Saharan Africa: 4.5

Higher birthrates are mostly found in the poorer countries, as the rate for "Heavily indebted poor countries" is 4.5 and for "Least developed countries" is 3.9. Plus, those they classify as "low income" had a 4.5 average birthrate whereas those who were "upper middle income" had an average of just 1.6. All of which leads to this ultimate population projection by the World Bank: "By 2100, 5 of the 10 most populated countries are projected to be in Africa."[46]

As we progress deeper into this century, the race will be on for developed nations as they compete against each other for immigrant talent. And those same competitors will likely invest in Africa to develop skilled workers for both there and abroad.

In Closing, the "War for Talent" Was a Snowball Fight

In 2001, a group of McKinsey consultants authored a book called *The War for Talent*.[47] I had just worked with two of those authors on a project with my then-current company, so I was eager to see what these same consultants had to say about talent. My copy still sits in the bookcase next to my desk.

The authors detailed initial doubts about using "war" in their title due to its militaristic tone, but later concluded their title "vividly captures the new realities of the talent market."

Ten years later, Gallup CEO Jim Clifton wrote another jobs-related book and named it *The Coming Jobs War*, describing his book this way:

> The war for global jobs is like World War II: a war for all the marbles. The global war for jobs determines the leader of the free world. If the United States allows China or any other country or region to out-enterprise it, out-job-create it, out-grow its GDP, everything changes. This is America's next war for everything.[48]

There are few companies I respect more than McKinsey and Gallup. I'm confident those same authors would agree that we are now facing a much higher, unprecedented wall regarding the absence of workers that will continue standing for the remainder of our lifetimes.

Five Summary Thoughts for the Next Twenty Years

1. There will be even fewer workers and more help-wanted signs, whether created by AI or magic markers, summarized by this US Census Bureau quote: "By 2034, we project that older adults will outnumber children for the first time in U.S. history."[49]

2. While most talk will be about worker *quantity*, worker *quality* will also take center stage as both will be required for businesses to stay in business.

3. Given young worker trendlines, retaining them for two years or even six months will require fresh thinking versus traditional employee surveys that lead to one-size-fits-all programs and thinking.

4. More immigrants will become visible on all job levels. Visit Toronto to envision this in a high-income, mainly English-speaking city.

5. Worker shortages will become the dominant driver of all economic trends by becoming the foundation for increased inflation, supply chain woes, and more because businesses cannot make products cost-effectively and on time without good workers.

2 ■ The Aha Moment of a Fix

In the early 1990s, I was a young HR buck working for a multistate regional banking company. My territory was the midsection of Florida, where we had about seventy branches, all overseen by a regional president. I'll refer to him as BD.

Each January, we held an annual Saturday meeting for about one hundred top-level managers. BD had risen up on the marketing side and had earned a strong community leadership presence throughout the Orlando and central Florida region, so as a marketeer this meeting was prime meat for him. Two other career achievements also weighed heavily into BD's management style, as he had been both an Air Force lieutenant and a college cheerleader. More on that later.

Of course, nametags and the rest had to be perfect, so planning seemed to be year-round. My main role was to draft a few speeches and rehearse those who had been anointed to take the podium.

Our corporate CEO, BD's boss, was always the final speaker, and the mystery among us planners was that we never knew what he would say, making the CEO's speech the annual meeting wild card. His words on a January Saturday in 1993 changed my life, and I can remember them distinctly:

> The difference between our company and our competitors is they are playing with veterans, and we are playing with rookies. Our greatest weakness throughout our company is our high employee turnover.

He then reached into his sport coat pocket and pulled out an 8-by-11 list he showed to his audience, saying this:

> You all probably don't know what your annual turnover is, but I do because I have each region's annual turnover for 1992 right here. And when I come to your monthly board meeting, I'll expect to hear an updated turnover report, and I'll also expect to hear that your turnover is getting better each month.

Sitting stunned, I was immediately handed a note from a fellow HR executive that read "Oh s__t," followed by three exclamation points.

The Never-Forget-Career-Changing Meeting

Forty-eight hours later on Monday morning, BD summoned me to his office. With quick delivery he repeated the CEO's comments and informed me that I was solely accountable for cutting turnover and must now report retention improvement each month. And because turnover was measurable, he would know if I was performing my job correctly.

I protested in a professional way, saying that each of us could make an identical list of those managers who repeatedly had the highest monthly turnover as well as the lowest employee engagement survey scores—but I had no authority to ask those managers to perform better. After a short exchange, BD rose from his chair to signal that our short meeting was coming to an end.

Our meeting, though, had one more twist. BD approached me until we stood facing each other, two tall men eighteen inches apart, and sought out the right closing words that would push me out of his office. Realizing nothing good was coming, I reminisced about BD acting out in lieutenant style by pointing his finger in managers' faces, yet I'd also seen that former cheerleader style where he had been demonstrably encouraging others to do better.

After about four tense seconds, BD smiled broadly and then said this: "I know you can do this, Dick Finnegan, in fact your middle name is now . . ." He snuck a peek toward the ceiling to decide what my new middle name would be, before shouting, *"Turnover! You are now Richard T. Finnegan!"*

The "T" was sung musically in three notes, hi-lo-hi, accompanied by his right arm rotating at a fast speed, cheerleader style.

I returned to my office blindsided by many thoughts, among them being *who am I going to tell this story to first*—though being a good HR pro, I kept the full story to myself.

A Legitimate Fear

After dinner that night I updated my résumé. My fear was double-edged as I had seen the strict lieutenant side of BD before, and I also knew we in HR had implemented every retention solution that a decade in HR had taught me. This list is common to all HR professionals and includes exit surveys, engagement surveys, salary surveys, benefits surveys—and probably even more surveys—accompanied by recognition events, career ladders, communications activities, and the rest.

Later that week, our top corporate HR executive flew in from headquarters, having been summoned by BD to "discuss my future." I later learned that on the same day BD changed my middle name, he later asked my peers if I should be fired.

Researchers say that those among us who are truly happy operate their lives with a defined set of mental and behavioral traits, one being that happy people see each event in their lives as both positive and negative, intertwined. That happy people stay emotionally steady by seeing advantages and disadvantages related to each individual life event, such that their ongoing happiness is never totally "tipped" by a good event or a bad one (e.g., "I got married so I'm forever happy" or

"I got divorced, and I'm doomed"). Until name-change Monday I had always liked every aspect of my job, but updating my résumé was followed by a long night trying to sleep. I saw no good in the bad.

The Never-Taught-in-HR Fix

Two days later I had lunch with good guy Dan, the executive who oversaw each of our seventy branches that contained nearly all of our employees. I told Dan my assignment and also the results of some homework I had done during the two days prior. Branch annual turnover was ranging from a high of 75 percent to a low of 15 percent. And there was no easy way to explain these differences.

I didn't realize then that we had the right conditions for a borderline-pristine academic study. Bank branches are nearly identical in that they have the same jobs, same pay, same benefits, same furniture, same products—as well as the same shingles, bricks, and signs—and their only significant variable is their manager. And as Dan and I studied the managers' names of the branches with the highest and lowest turnover, we readily saw that each manager's level of turnover pretty much correlated with their people-management reputations, whether good or not so good.

At the end of lunch, we made a profound decision: *We would assign each manager an annual retention goal and expect them to meet it.* My job would be to track each manager's goal progress and distribute a report each month on how many employees they had lost during that month, the number they had lost for that twelve-month period, and the limited number they could lose ongoing to achieve their annual goal. I would add to the report any notable actions any manager took that were intended to reduce their turnover.

What's remarkable is what Dan and I decided *not* to do. No new supervisory training, no updated onboarding, no new hiring tools— and of course no salary bumps or shiny new benefits. And we disregarded past engagement survey and exit survey results. We committed on that day that our cutting turnover to meet the CEO's command was in the hands of the managers of each branch. And maybe my future with the company was too.

Looking back, the seismic change was that we moved retention accountability from HR to operations. This was based on instinct at the time; I later learned we were right in line with the academic research.

A few days later, we brought our CFO into the fold by asking for help with calculating the dollar value of losing a teller. Our resulting amount was $4,413.

The First Road Trip

Dan and I scheduled a series of branch manager meetings to announce our employee retention improvement plan beginning in the Leesburg, Florida, branch, knowing we would inhale the wooden smell of the obligatory fresh mulch in all planted areas by the front door, a commonplace practice for an executive visit.

With a crowd of about twenty branch managers, I began the meeting by displaying branch turnover trends and our newly determined cost of teller turnover—all via overheads back then. Dan followed with the kicker—that our sole solution was that each branch manager in the room would be held accountable to achieve an annual retention goal.

For the managers, Dan's punchline was more of a gut punch. After about seven seconds of silence, a manager in the back stood up and said these words, verbatim: "Do you mean that you expect us to keep our people, that this goal thing is about us and not about HR or anyone else? And you're not going to raise pay?"

Dan answered that he was asking each manager to improve turnover by 10 percent, and that they could blame the remaining 90 percent on pay, benefits, HR, or even their dog if they wanted. That ended any further discussion. Word spread immediately to the other fifty managers, so our remaining meetings were short. Many managers called me in the ensuing days to privately complain, and I recall the word "sucks" was prominent in their lexicon. For example, "the pay sucks," "the benefits suck," and maybe "you suck" after they hung up the phone.

But who could blame them? Our entire culture had driven the belief that employees work mainly for pay, and that HR should ensure we hire the best ones followed by leveraging our salary and benefits package to keep them. Branch managers were in charge of numbers like loans and deposits, plus managing customer complaints. And joining Rotary.

The Results . . . and the End

Turnover fell by 19 percent over the next ninety days, and as a result we saved over $4 million in teller retention alone. And we found that more employees were staying because their managers were, well, just being *nicer*. They opened their previously closed doors, asked how little Johnny's little league game was, and told employees they were doing their jobs well. And they probably hired much more carefully because new hires had proven to be the most vulnerable to leaving.

Toward the end of the year, BD announced that we had licked turnover, so he stopped the monthly reporting against goals. Turnover immediately increased because pressure was shifted to some other important metric, and our retention initiative was erased.

Here's a Florida analogy. If you hold a beachball underwater and then let it go, it surges through the water and flies into the air. That's what our turnover did because we stopped tracking it, and by doing so we lost the benefit of retention accountability.

Now was the time to rethink that good-and-bad-intertwined thing. I had been frightened into searching for a way-out-of-the-box solution to cut employee turnover. The solution worked, my job was safe, and I had lessons learned to take forward with me.

Going Global

Sometime later, I became involved with the American Bankers Association (ABA), teaching HR courses in their various certification programs across several college campuses with my bank's permission to do so. Eventually my ABA manager left to take a leadership role with KPMG's international consulting division and invited me to join her. I reluctantly passed, seeing no way to be responsible to my family while flying across oceans. But she then mentioned doing so part-time. BD had recently retired, and my new executive was encouraging, so we made an agreement where I could do both jobs.

Over the next two years I worked in various locations in Asia, Europe, and South America, as well as Siberia, where I rode the Trans-Siberian Railway from Novosibirsk to Omsk. My role was to teach management courses of my choosing and sometimes coach executive teams, accompanied by translators of course. Employee retention accountability was front and center in all coursework and coaching, and over time those executives who spoke English kept me apprised of their downward-trending turnover.

Before Digging for Research

My international work required new skills, some creativity, and mostly independence, which together made my day job far less rewarding. Newfound confidence had grown an entrepreneurial seed that I could never have imagined before, having lived a risk-adverse life that resulted from being parented by two loving people whose life experiences began with the Great Depression and were then interrupted by the terror of World War II.

So, after eighteen years, I resigned my bank job to make a go at becoming an employee retention consultant. On one hand, I had no competition because no one had ever risked doing this before, but hustle brought me clients, beginning with Hilton's call centers and growing to include the CIA.

Most interesting was AngloGold Ashanti, one of the largest gold-mining companies in the world. *Training & Development* magazine had run a story on my work that wound up in their company library in Johannesburg, South Africa. This led to me making several on-site visits to reduce miner turnover, which required me to descend four kilometers deep into a mine that has been measured to be the deepest on earth.

Then one day, I was keynoting a conference in San Francisco when a woman approached me to ask if I wanted to write a book. She subsequently sent me a contract that indicated I would write forty thousand words, causing me to call her with shaky intimidation. She suggested I tell my travel stories, but I knew I was at heart a one-fix pony. I had built my reputation on leadership accountability for employee retention, which would never be enough to meaningfully fill a top-selling book.

Again, I faced a crossroads. Could I invent a comprehensive solution to cut employee turnover, chasing my professional passion into a legitimate profession? The encouraging perspective was that I had centered on a business area that had never been fully explored before—a green field of sorts. Accountants, lawyers, and other professionals were entering their professions after having been trained in proven, effective processes they could follow to do their jobs well. Yet there had never been a proven process to cut employee turnover, and I had the opportunity to develop one.

The Top Five Lessons I Learned from This Experience

1. Everything HR taught me about reducing turnover was wrong, or at least incomplete.
2. The best and easiest-to-implement solution is to hold first-line leaders accountable to retention goals.
3. Yet it is a formidable challenge to convince company executives that any retention solution should involve managers on any level rather than relying on HR.
4. Manager retention accountability improves turnover across many cultures and languages, so this solution is universal.
5. My own professional fears were reversed by successes, a lesson I've taken throughout my life.

3 ■ What the Experts Tell Us

Looking back, our "cut bank turnover" solution seemed too simple. We had instructed managers to achieve a monthly retention goal and most of them achieved it. Immediately. Our aggregate turnover fell off a cliff, fast. And this happened with little coaching.

There were references to our monthly leader retention report in team and individual manager meetings, but I can't recall one tension-filled discussion. We had placed a laser focus on one number each month so that, for example, a manager could lose two employees and still achieve their monthly turnover goal, but they could lose no more than that number.

Another reason that branch banks posed as ideal study locations was that in most locations there was one manager who oversaw ten to twenty employees. In larger branches there might have been a head teller between the manager and the teller team, but all saw the appointed branch manager as their boss. And to be clear, we had implemented no new HR initiatives of any sort, leaving the managers on their islands to make or break their goals. We had offered no new hiring solutions either, though the managers were likely more careful about their new-hire decisions.

The bottom line was that our managers were making their own discretionary choices as to how to manage better and how to get closer to their teams, with no training and no outside help. Every single manager action that impacted employee retention was happening by the choice and native skills of each manager, within the walls of their own branch building.

With that scenario now long in the rearview mirror, the question becomes: Did we get lucky, or was there then and does there continue to be a body of research that supports this approach?

Introducing Professor Kevin Murphy

Drafting that first book—with its forty-thousand-word requirement—caused me to step up my game. I knew I needed academic help. Penn State was my academic home, having earned two degrees there, and their Industrial and Organizational Psychology Department was consistently rated among the top five in the country. The university's website told me that a Professor Kevin Murphy had a special interest in employee turnover.

Kevin took me on as a distant semi-student who paid no tuition and wanted no diploma, sending me weekly emails citing existing and new academic studies that impacted employee turnover. Many were dissertations that added a brick to the retention model I was building. One such brick was that top performers outperformed average performers by four to one.[1] I'll expand on this finding later by asking how effective can employee surveys be when all responses are anonymous, including those from the very employees you can least afford to lose.

Over several months, I filled notepad after notepad with scribbles from Kevin-sent studies that transformed me from a one-horse consultant into a comprehensive, thinking constructor of a full employee retention solution. I also became a "data dog," a continuous tracker of academic research. Let's now address what that research tells us about how to cut employee turnover by asking the following questions:

1. How much do first-line leaders impact employee turnover?
2. How important is it that first-line leaders develop trust with each individual employee in order to improve employee retention?

First-Line Leaders' Impact on Turnover and Engagement

Gallup's world-renowned research forms the largest body of data focused on both employee engagement and employee retention. Furthermore, Gallup consistently updates its reporting, and here are its most recent findings during the post-pandemic era that relate to the impact of first-line leaders on retention:

- The leading reason employees gave for leaving their employer is related to "employee engagement and culture" (47 percent).[2] Gallup cites three specific inclusions under that heading, which are (1) advancement and development opportunities, (2) not being treated with respect, and (3) unrealistic job expectations and responsibilities.
- In a related study, Gallup tells us that a full 42 percent of employee exits could have been prevented by their manager or their organization if managers scheduled enough individual meetings to learn what their employees need.[3] Gallup offers these quotes as examples of reasons why employees stayed based on meetings with their managers versus those who didn't meet with their managers and therefore left:
  - "Treated me with respect and showed concern for my wellbeing . . ."
  - "Allowed me autonomy to do my job, helped me in a path to advance my career . . ."
  - "Recognized my contributions to the team . . ."
- In an earlier study, Gallup reported that at least 75 percent of the reasons for voluntary turnover can be influenced by

managers, finding that people leave companies because of factors that filter through the local work environment.[4]

Most meaningful is the subtitle of Gallup's classic book titled *It's the Manager*, which is *Gallup Finds the Quality of Managers and Team Leaders Is the Single Biggest Factor in Your Organization's Long-Term Success.*[5] "Team leaders" is the new term here, included to emphasize the importance of the very lowest rung of first-line leaders who most interact with employees by training them, coaching them, providing feedback to them, and praising them. Two recent clients come to mind, both in manufacturing: In Company A, the top executive made the unilateral decision that team leaders would own retention accountability; in Company B, retention accountability was placed at the supervisor level, a higher and more distant level from the employees working on the manufacturing floor.

Which decision was better? And did that decision matter a little or a lot? The organization that leveraged team leaders cut turnover by greater than 30 percent, while the other company saw much smaller reductions. And the reason why is that for both companies their team leaders were the actual first-line supervisors, regardless of their titles and whether they were classified as exempt or nonexempt. This reinforces that the leaders who have the most impact on retention are those who work most closely daily with your employees.

Gallup is clearly pointing its research-based finger toward first-line leaders in the above examples. The first two studies stress the importance of employees being treated with respect, gaining recognition, chasing development opportunities, and having job autonomy—all core job responsibilities for first-line leaders. The third study defines the results we saw in each of our bank branches, that "people leave companies because of factors that filter through the local work environment." Those branch managers were indeed the number one players in our efforts to improve employee retention. They always had been, throughout the decades of HR interventions that brought little strength and little impact to actually cut employee turnover. And the full title of *It's the Manager* emphasizes the great retention power of the lowest possible leadership title: team leader.

More on First-Line Leaders' Retention Power

Here are additional examples of well-developed research that further proclaim first-line leaders' power to retain their teams.

According to Development Dimensions International (DDI), a full 57 percent of employees have quit one or more jobs because of bad bosses. In a related study, Kenexa surveyed over one thousand employees who had voluntarily left organizations, asking about their fit with supervisors as well as their satisfaction with pay, benefits, learning, development, and advancement. In all instances, employees' opinions were "mediated," or influenced, by relationships these employees had with their supervisors. The study concluded by saying, *"Offering a higher salary or development/advancement opportunities may not be enough to retain employees."*[6] This study found that how employees see their relationship with their first-line supervisor directly influences how they feel about other aspects of their jobs. Feel good about supervisor, feel good about pay. Dislike supervisor, feel bad about benefits. I would have written the conclusion differently: *First-line supervisors are therefore the prism, the lens through which employees decide how they feel about your company and all that you offer them.*

In another example, *Harvard Business Review* reported the following:

> The data suggests that leadership matters as never before—not just at the C-suite level but also at the front lines where managers really determine how organizational culture feels for employees. For example, there can be vast differences in caregiver morale in two patient care units that are physically adjacent to each other but have different nurse managers.[7]

While this report is specific to healthcare, its comparison of two different levels of first-line leaders' compassion drives home the extreme impact of leadership at the supervisory level.

In a previous book, I detailed the connection between first-line leaders and retention with case studies of Salary.com, the Healthcare Advisory Board, Monster.com, the Saratoga Institute, and the National Education Association.[8] Teacher turnover has been and will continue to be a major obstacle for improving our children's education, with blame appropriately thrown toward universally low teacher pay. But we learn in the National Education Association study that principals have such a strong influence as first-line supervisors that they can bring personal power to retain those teachers regardless of their pay, with one teacher saying, "I would follow my principal to a shed to teach."[9]

Our previously stated question to answer during this section was: How much do first-line leaders impact employee turnover? The jury is in, and their verdict is clear: *First-line leaders have the greatest of all impacts on how long employees stay with their organizations.* Let's next address the essential skill they must develop in order to do so.

The Neuroscience of Trust

Most of us cut to the chase when reading academic studies, but this one deserves our closest attention. Paul Zak is a Claremont Graduate University professor who has an eye-of-the-tiger drive to take his research to the deepest level. Zak has identified the correlation between high trust and high retention, along with several other productivity variables, and here's the remarkable way he got there.

Way back in 2001, Zak derived a mathematical relationship between trust and economic performance, yet he felt his hands were tied because he couldn't answer why it is that two people trust each other in the first place. So, he and his research team began a fifteen-year quest to answer this question and more by doing the following:

- The team already knew that rodents showed an increase in a brain chemical called oxytocin when they felt safe to approach another animal.
- They then devised an exercise where humans could make a choice whether or not to trust another human, and drew blood from participants' arms before and after making their trusting or nontrusting choice.
- Those who made trusting choices showed greater increases in oxytocin.
- Then, to double-check their findings, the team administered synthetic doses of oxytocin via nasal spray to a

control group and found that group to be even more
trusting, concluding that oxytocin appears to do just one
thing: reduce the fear of trusting a stranger.

- Additional studies found that oxytocin increases a person's
empathy, that stress can reduce the amount of oxytocin in
the body, and other reasons why trust levels vary across
individuals and situations.

When Zak applied his research to organizations, those organizations reported higher productivity, more engagement, and most importantly for us, more *loyalty* as 50 percent more employees planned to stay with their employers over the next year. I'll present Zak's specific individual managerial actions that led to this improvement later in Chapter 5.[10]

A Theory You Can Count On

My many years of focusing strictly on reducing employee turnover has led to me this unproven-but-I'd-bet-my-pool-table-on-it belief:

A sure indicator of whether an employee is thinking of quitting is what they talk about over dinner.

Think about it. If you could place hidden microphones under each of your employees' dinner tables, you could toss engagement surveys, exit surveys, focus groups, and all of those other interventions that we've been led to believe tell us what matters most to them.

Dinner conversations open doors to what really matters to people. They have been used for decades as settings for movies, plays, sitcoms, and *Saturday Night Live* sketches. This is where family members must make eye contact and communicate as their only other activity is putting food in their mouths. Dinner is when we take breaks from staring at our screens and actually interact with each other. For many of us, it's the only built-in social time with family members or those we are closest to.

Let's expand "dinner time" to any of the times and places where we are greeted by others after leaving work. Whereas dinner time is a good fit for those who work traditionally scheduled 9–5 weekday jobs, others arrive at home on different schedules. Or they arrive somewhere else—at a restaurant, bar, gym—wherever they seek end-of-workday solace to transition their minds and bodies to another place. It is then when we talk with others about our just-completed workdays.

We also talk to *ourselves* about those just-completed workdays on our commutes home in our cars, buses, trains, or transitioning from room to room if we work at home. These way-home-daily-reviews are unstructured and often unwelcome because we are glad our workday is over. Yet we can't quite turn off our minds, can't immediately decompress, because those psychic interruptions dominate our thoughts. They are not built around the sequential schedules of our day but are instead about that one day's emotional spikes, both good and bad.

Move past this psychological drama for a moment and think about what each of your employees actually talk about over dinner. If you were secretly there, what might you hear about their workdays that might be different from the structured questionnaires you provide to them via various types of employee surveys?

Why We Are Less Emotionally Intelligent Over Dinner

Like all humans, your employees are emotional beings first and rational beings second. This is the foundation of emotional intelligence. Every bit of incoming information we gather via our five senses enters our brains first by way of our limbic system—the emotional center located at the top of our spinal cords.[11] If we walk by a garden and smell flowers, our brain says, "That smells good," with no deeper delving into *why* the flowers smell good—they just do.

That same information eventually finds its way to the front of the brain, where our emotional responses are mediated by our rational ones. This is where the brain determines what colors the flowers are, how many there are, or why they smell so good. This perspective switch might take milliseconds in the example of flowers or hours, days, or even weeks as we eventually view complex issues more rationally. Put very simply, how soon information makes its way from the emotional brain to the rational brain determines how emotionally intelligent we are.

We're likely to have less than optimal emotional intelligence immediately after work, when both our bodies and minds are exhausted. We're also interacting with people where we feel safer than we do with our colleagues from work, be they family members, friends, or the person sitting next to us at a bar or restaurant. These interactions are happening while our brains are tired, so any transfer from our emotional brain to our rational brain is unlikely to occur until the next morning or even later.

After work is therefore when we talk about how we *feel* about our day. We share stories—about a satisfied customer, a jerk coworker, a rare compliment from the boss—and do so emotionally, sometimes with raised voices and vigorous gestures. And our emotions from each day could theoretically be scored on a 1 to 10 scale with 10 meaning we love our job and 1 meaning we hate it.

An important question emerges from the above discussion: Are we more likely to disengage from or quit our jobs based on our *emotional* responses or our *rational* ones? My guess is we disengage and quit most often based on our emotional responses because every work-related input must pass through that mind-gate first. Some of our emotional responses never transform into rational thought, especially the ones the brain generates over and over. And emotions stick with most of us for a very long time.

We Know What Your Employees Talk About Over Dinner

Experience has taught me that these are the main things people talk about over dinner:

1. Bosses
2. Colleagues
3. Duties

Unless an exceptional event happens on a particular day, this is your employees' daily mantra that they express to themselves and others: bosses, colleagues, duties. And who has the most influence over what your employees talk about over dinner? *Their direct supervisors do.* Your first-line supervisors have the most influence over how your employees talk about *them* over dinner, how your employees talk about their *colleagues* over dinner, and how your employees talk about their *duties* over dinner.

The connection between your supervisors' influence on what their employees say about *them* over dinner is obvious. When employees complain about a coworker, their baseline complaint is about why their supervisors don't confront that employee's performance or fire them. And when employees complain about poor equipment, too much paperwork, or other processes that are parts of their everyday jobs, they distribute blame back on their supervisors for that, too.

As we've now learned, most employees' opinions about their supervisors are identical to their opinions about their companies. Their relationships with their supervisors are as far as they can see up the chain.

How do we know? First, because of thousands of Stay Interview results, which I'll discuss more in Chapter 6. And second because of the immense amount of research that tells us *the number one reason employees stay or leave, or engage or disengage, is based on how much they trust their immediate supervisors.*

Rarely does a good employee quit because of just one event. Later I'll discuss research that shows hardly anyone quits for pay alone. *Most employees quit because of a thousand paper cuts* caused by the same relationship squabbles or the same work incidents that repeat themselves over time.

The Pet Insurance Joke

When speaking at conferences, I usually toss in this laugh line:

> Whenever employees are asked over dinner, "How was your day, dear?" no one ever answers, "My day was OK, but I just wish we had pet insurance."

If that same employee is feeling a lack of recognition at work, they don't say, "Just hopin' we have Employee Appreciation Day this year" or "Just three years to go before I get that company clock." Or that their department should have more events with food. Similarly, no one thinks the solution to poor communications is to have more meetings; or that tuition reimbursement or job posting can solve career development on their own.

Considering what you just read about immediate supervisors driving retention, the references here to pet insurance, Employee Appreciation Day, company clocks, and free food all seem worthy of ridicule. But many organizations actually believe things like this drive employees to work harder and stay longer. The point is not to eliminate these one-size-fits-all programs but instead to lower your own expectations that they will generate a lasting impact on your employees' engagement or retention.

A Real-Life Example

A few years ago, I was addressing the top twenty-five executives of a pharmaceutical company in California. When I told the pet insurance joke, one executive took such offense that he stood up among his peers to exclaim that he'd told his employees to never talk about work at home and that their homes were havens for work–life balance, so he was certain that such a dinner exchange had never happened among his employees.

My first instinct was to recognize him as the one in a thousand executives who cared so much. Instead, I took a chance and asked the full group to answer honestly whether they had talked about their boss over dinner just in the past week. The hands of the other twenty-four executives went straight up.

For perspective, these were top-level executives who live in big homes. Their CEO was present, and he too raised his arm. If these dinner exchanges are happening at your company's highest level, even occasionally, then they are certainly happening down at the entry level, too.

I write a weekly *Targeting Turnover* blog that is distributed widely and is sometimes referenced by major publications. *Forbes* repeated the above story and then added their own editorial opinion: "Even those of us who love hard data must acknowledge this, which reinforces the old adage that people don't quit jobs, they quit bosses. And it is those bosses they talk about over dinner."[12]

I tell this story when training managers to conduct Stay Interviews and conclude by saying, "You are on the menu every night. But you get to decide what they say about you by your everyday actions as a supervisor."

Three Summary Thoughts on What the Experts Tell Us

Putting all of these data and discussions into summary form provides us with the following statements of fact, and these become the basis—the spine—of my employee retention solution:

1. The number one reason employees stay or leave, or for that matter engage or disengage, is how much they trust their immediate supervisors.
2. This *does not* mean that each time an employee quits it is because she doesn't trust her boss—employees quit for many reasons—though that might well be the reason.
3. It *does* mean that each individual leader becomes your very best employee retention solution.

What are the revelations that come with declaring each individual leader as your best employee retention solution? It means those solutions that do not involve your first-line leaders take a back seat—a far back seat—in your efforts to cut turnover. That bag of solutions includes the usual outcomes of employee surveys or other companies' retention "best practices" like improved onboarding, recognition events, CEO videos, annual service awards, most employee benefits, and any events with food. I will address the relative importance of additional pay below in Chapter 10.

These one-size-fits-all programs will have little impact on whether any employee stays or leaves your organization, and their impact lessens even more when employees work remotely or hundreds of miles from your headquarters office. You can certainly continue doing them, but please reduce your expectation that they will have a significant impact on improving employee retention.

For a concluding thought, here's a quote from Marcus Buckingham and Curt Coffman's groundbreaking book *First, Break All the Rules*:

> The talented employee may join a company because of its charismatic leaders, its generous benefits, and its world-class training programs, but how long that employee stays and how productive he is while he is there is determined by his relationship with his immediate supervisor.[13]

4 ■ Gluing Solutions Together into Finnegan's Arrow

Let's begin this discussion with a two-question exercise. The first question seems easy, but it might be hard; the second question will lead to quick answers for almost every situation—except for the situation that is core to this book.

Question #1: What is the absolutely most important metric for your organization?

- For starters, if you are in healthcare, your answer might be patient satisfaction. Or it might be average daily census. Or should you work in critical care, it might be the number of patients who survive to return home.
- If in manufacturing, your answer could be the number of products produced in an hour or a day or another period of time, or perhaps the error rate that leads to revenue-draining returns. Or worker safety might be near the top.

And what about goal achievement for the salespeople who sell your products?

- In call centers, your answer might be average call time or percentage of calls resolved at the first level. Or whether your agents achieve a certain level of caller satisfaction.
- In financial services, the answer might be total annual revenue or percentage of increase in loans or deposits. Or what about your share of the market, locally or overall?
- In social services, is it dollars raised or the number of clients to whom you provide services? And what about the quality of those services?
- If in a publicly traded company, there's a good chance your answer will involve the price of your stock. And your answer will differ depending on whether you work in the corporate office or in a subsidiary.

I spent the first part of my career working for two major universities. How important were the number of student registrations that brought in the cash versus the number of graduates who contributed to society? Or the faculty achievements that seemed so important even though they never felt like they impacted the quality of classroom instruction?

For many of us, Question #1 is not easy. But please take your best try at establishing an answer and move on to the second question.

Question #2: What single job in your organization is most responsible for achieving your absolutely most important metric?

The easy out here is to target the top, to say the CEO or the local plant manager has the most responsibility. But please dig more deeply by considering jobs that are closer each day to the most important metric you chose above, such as the following:

- Salespeople are the obvious answer if your most important metric is sales.
- Development directors matter most if your nonprofit's most important metric is achieving fundraising goals.

- Loan officers are the winning answer if your financial services profitability leans mostly on increasing your loan portfolio.

The job you select represents the employees who are closest to the action for achieving your company's most important metric, so they become the trigger for your company's success or failure.

Application to Employee Retention

How then does this exercise connect to employee retention? The connection to the first question—about the most important metric—ties back to the information presented in Chapter 1. Given that we are facing the "Great Gully," which will cause the sheer number of additions to our workforce to drop off a cliff for the coming twenty years and longer, I urge you to add "reducing employee turnover" to your top-three metrics. The obvious reason why is that you cannot execute your organization's top objectives without retaining your best workers. The not-so-obvious reason is because most companies today claim employee retention is extremely important but turn their attention to other metrics with their day-to-day focus. And they fail to do the right things to improve employee retention at all.

Question #2, however, opens the door to the most important message of this book: *The single greatest reason why organizations cannot reduce employee turnover is because they either hold the wrong people accountable for it or they hold no one accountable for it at all.*

The Five Components of Finnegan's Arrow

The Finnegan's Arrow model, as seen in Figure 6, connects together all of the concepts mentioned so far that have proven to successfully reduce turnover, some based on research and some based on practice. While Finnegan's Arrow presents five components that happen sequentially—dollars, goals, Stay Interviews, forecasts, and accountability—its prime job is to provide leaders on all levels with the tools to help them retain their teams, along with the required accountability for doing so.

FINNEGAN'S ARROW®

Figure 6: Finnegan's Arrow

Component #1: Dollars

Consider the absurdity that employee turnover drives so much impact on profitability, yet there is no universally accepted method for measuring its cost. Or that finance professionals open their screens each day to search the same reports over and over in hopes of finding a quarter-in-the-couch new idea to save a penny on a dollar—all while millions of dollars are going out the door around the corner in HR because of turnover.

FINNEGAN'S ARROW

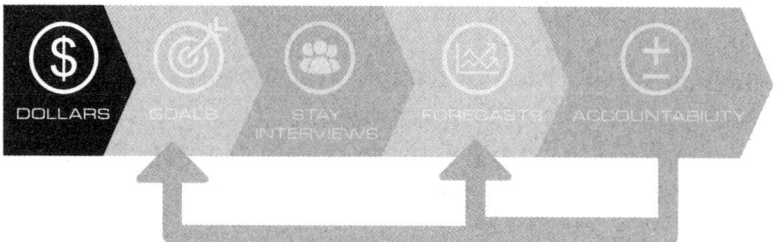

"Around the corner in HR" is most companies' perspective that reducing employee turnover is an HR problem but not an executive problem. Finance people are doing what their MBA programs taught them to do, where there is little if any training on costing or solving employee turnover as a major business issue. A few companies have adopted one of several "best practice" ideas that turnover costs 50 percent of an employees' annual pay or whatever. But no CFO will ever accept that as a serious metric of turnover's real cost.

Generally Accepted Accounting Principles (GAAP) are standards that public companies in the United States must follow when reporting their financial information. Googling "GAAP and employee turnover" yields a few studies on the cost of losing a CEO or CFO, but nothing on the impact of total employee turnover on other key business metrics. It's as though turnover doesn't really exist in our organizations, that it has no presence on Accounting's screens. Yet Gallup estimates the cost of voluntary turnover to American businesses is a staggering $1 trillion—every year.[1]

Component #1, then, addresses this shortcoming. The *second reason* for costing turnover is to establish an ongoing measurement to be expressed in dollars, but the more important *first reason* is to dump a bucket of ice water over executives' heads so that they see employee retention as an extremely costly business issue rather than an HR issue.

Our company has invented a no-cost online algorithm that you can use to measure the cost of turnover by job, and I'll provide a way for you to access this calculator near the end of this book.

Let me offer several tips for using our calculator here:

- Start with the job that is the most painful job for turnover in terms of frequency or impact on other key metrics.
- Ideal participants for using the algorithm include a manager for that job, someone who recruits for that job, and a finance representative who can provide a few numbers and also verify the outcome's accuracy to your CFO—or just invite your CFO.
- *Lost productivity* is the calculator's most important feature.

The few existing turnover cost calculators measure costs similar to those used in measuring the cost of hire, such as costs for recruiting, onboarding, training, and any required materials or uniforms. The far greater cost for turnover, though, is the lost productivity in two instances: while the job is open and while the new hire ramps up. As just one example, a recent study details the hundreds of millions of dollars lost by a consumer electronics company due to production errors caused by employee turnover—and costs such as these will never appear in a standard cost-per-hire model or a simplified "50 percent of annual salary" calculation.[2]

No turnover cost calculator is complete unless it includes a mathematical way to measure these lost productivity costs. Our calculator captures these costs in a unique way that ultimately generates the dollar value for each job's daily contribution to revenue and then multiplies that daily cost by the number of days the job stays open and half the number of days the new hire ramps up, acknowledging that the new hire contributes more each day during the ramp-up period.

Here are just a few of the dollar-cost-per-exits our clients have calculated:

- Nurse: $42,131
- Truck loader/unloader: $4,955
- Call center representative: $29,447
- Physician: $225,808
- Truck driver: $21,221
- Software engineer: $131,290
- Forklift driver: $10,742
- Manufacturing entry-level: $5,518

The reaction of an aerospace company CFO was like no other. He reluctantly joined in to participate in the calculation and ultimately agreed to the cost for losing an engineer to be $121,500. He called me early the next morning from work to say he hadn't been able to sleep. He told me that with some extrapolation he had discovered that his company's turnover cost was their second-highest cost, placing that cost ahead of the properties and materials required for his company to build rockets.

Some savvy client companies make their turnover cost study far more comprehensive by including all jobs in their calculations, thereby becoming able to assign one cost to their company's turnover for each month or for a full year. The resulting chart looks like that in Figure 7, which uses a healthcare company as an example.

The methodology for calculating comprehensive turnover cost is this:

Hospital Example: Twelve-Month Costs, Five Job Bands

Job Group	Example Jobs	Cost/Exit ($)	Cost/12 Months ($)
Nonskilled	Environmental service, food services, admittance representative	$8,503	$255,090
Skilled Hourly	Patient care, phlebotomist secretary	$12,627	$568,215
Licensed Hourly	Rehab therapy, radio, tech, respiratory therapists	$20,388	$428,128
Nurses	Inpatient nurses, emergency nurses, surgical nurses	$46,250	$2,350,00
Exempt	Managers, directors, case managers	$57,857	$694,284
TOTAL			$4,295,717

Figure 7: Comprehensive Annual Cost of Turnover
Source: C-Suite Analytics and Richard P. Finnegan.

1. Group all of your organization's jobs into fewer than ten bands, each band based on similarities of job skills, job level, time to fill, annual salary, and whether the job includes extra payments such as for hiring bonuses, performance bonuses, or stock.
2. Then calculate the cost of turnover for one job in each band and apply that cost to all jobs in the band.
3. Record the number of exits within each band over each month or year and then summarize your organization's total turnover cost for that period.

No turnover calculator will capture all turnover costs, with just one example being turnover's impact on worker injuries. And calculating turnover cost is only worth the work to do so if your finance team continues to report ongoing turnover costs and aggregated savings for years to come.

Component #2: Goals

During a recent conference presentation, I polled the audience on who in their organizations was accountable for reducing employee turnover. After soliciting potential responses for executives, managers, and HR, their overwhelming response was "all of the above," to which I replied "all of the above" is code for no one is responsible—that sometimes the concept of "we're all in this together" leads to the absence of individual accountability and nothing more.

FINNEGAN'S ARROW

Peter Drucker pioneered the goal concept with his term "management by objectives" (MBO), and US firms are mostly excellent at identifying goal metrics, even if they do so only at budget time. But as demonstrated by the two-question exercise at the start of this chapter, properly designed metrics and accountabilities for employee retention are rare.

Our goal-setting process requires the same level of pre-work as does costing turnover. We ask clients for their turnover data for the previous twelve months and subsequently present charts for turnover by job, leader, shift, length-of-service, and other factors. From here we identify and target two goals:

- Goal #1 is to reduce overall employee turnover by 20 percent, meaning, for example, if turnover is 50 percent, then reduce it to 40 percent.
- Goal #2 is to improve new-hire retention by 20 percent during the new-hire period when turnover is highest, so, for example, a new-hire goal might be to improve first-sixty-day retention to 80 percent.

Here are important considerations regarding Goal #1:

- Simple is better, meaning that one goal for all jobs and all shifts is ideal.
- At the same time, the goal must be fair, so sometimes multiple goals make sense, with a good example being late shifts having higher turnover because of the less attractive hours of the shift.
- The percentage goal becomes clearer when translated into a numerical goal. For example, in order to reduce annual turnover by 20 percent, we can lose no more than X employees per month.
- Both voluntary and involuntary exits must count because both cost money and we want no debates about which exits are in and out of our count.
- Hospitals provide a strong example of where the goal might apply to only one key job, such as nurses, because nursing turnover is the most costly; the same might apply to agents in call centers.

Important considerations for Goal #2 are:

- For industries with high new-hire turnover, winning the new-hire goal will propel you toward winning the annual turnover goal.
- Studying your turnover by length of service will lead you to identify the new-hire goal period.
- Our clients usually "spotlight" the new hires who are in the new-hire goal period, sometimes with physical distinctions like colored arm bands or helmets, and other times by locking in frequent meetings to discuss how to advance each new hire to the end of the goal period.
- When the data are unclear, choose a shorter new-hire goal period in order to ensure greater spotlighting focus.

Spotlighting new hires to drive their retention through the complete new-hire goal period increases the likelihood that the goal will be met. One shipping company established a thirty-day new-hire goal, so we placed banners throughout the facility that read "How're Your First 30 Days?" accompanied with green armbands, which caused veteran employees to ask that same question when they spotted the green armband on new hires. A manufacturing company pulled all managers into a weekly meeting to specifically discuss how those managers would retain new hires for their sixty-day new-hire goal period, and during the same meeting confront which employees they had lost prior to sixty days and why.

Having completed the pre-work for determining turnover's costs and likely goals, we meet with executive teams to gain their commitment for our turnover cost calculation, the agreed-upon retention goals, and the dollars to be saved once the goals have been achieved. This process moves retention accountability from HR to operations—where it has always belonged.

Component #3: Stay Interviews

Stay Interviews as they are known today were invented during the seventh inning of a major league baseball game in San Diego's Petco Park, circa 2011. A publisher friend suggested then that I build on a concept I had presented previously in order to tell the reading public that first-line managers could conduct these types of meetings with their direct reports to build trust, cut turnover, and improve employee engagement. The resulting book was *The Power of Stay Interviews* (2012, rev. 2018), which for years sat atop the best-selling books for the Society for Human Resource Management, the global HR society.

FINNEGAN'S ARROW

The concept of Stay Interviews is simple. If the top reason employees stay or leave is how much they trust their first-line supervisors, I felt it was incumbent on me to develop an *interactive* way that each supervisor could learn why each member of their team stays, might leave, and what that supervisor can do to keep them.

An alternative invention could have been standardized trust training, where each participant learns, let's say, seven principles of trust, then develops a personalized checklist of related behaviors they will improve. Participants leave the training having committed to making those improvements. But this description defines many types of supervisory training that have little or no ultimate impact because they don't require post-training actions to practice what the participants had learned.

Much of the research provided in Chapter 3 calls out for the invention of Stay Interviews as a spot-on match—recall that Gallup found that a full 42 percent of employee exits could have been prevented by their organization or their manager, who did not schedule enough individual meetings to learn what their employees need.[3] This eventually led to Gallup developing what appears to be their own version, which they refer to as "stay conversations," in 2021.[4]

One might argue that we are already asking employees what they want given the plethora of employee engagement surveys, pulse surveys, and exit surveys. But the reality is that these asking methods have long been flawed, and, as most employees have told us, their track record for actually solving the very problems they identify is weak.

I'll address both how to facilitate Stay Interviews effectively and the shortcomings of employee surveys later in this book.

Component #4: Forecasting

The idea of supervisors forecasting how long each employee will stay was born in a client meeting many years ago when we were whiteboarding ways to put teeth into managers feeling driven to achieve their new-hire retention goals. Implementing this idea brought such powerful authority to our total solutions that we made forecasting a permanent inclusion for all supervisors and for all of their employees. Forecasting works like this:

- Supervisors forecast how long each employee will stay after that employee's first Stay Interview.
- The forecasting method is deliberately easy to grasp as (a) green indicates that employee will stay with your company for at least one year, (b) yellow indicates that employee will leave in six to twelve months whether voluntarily or otherwise, and (c) red indicates that employee will exit within six months.
- Supervisors should use all of the knowledge they have when forecasting, for recently conducted Stay Interviews, ongoing indications of high or low job interest, or even high absences or other performance issues.
- The supervisor may change the forecast as often as merited—every day if there is reason to do so.

FINNEGAN'S ARROW

The greatest of the many forecasting benefits is that supervisors must make a choice, committing themselves to an important metric for which they will henceforth be accountable regarding each member of their team. Asking the five Stay Interview questions, which I'll present in Chapter 6, and then listening intently to the employee's responses is one form of commitment, but choosing which forecast color is most applicable for each employee represents a *documented* commitment, and therefore deeper thought.

We leverage this commitment and its resulting accountability in several ways, starting with our standard plea of "Don't lose a green." Supervisors are usually optimistic at first because they have entered into new layers of their relationships with their individual employees, and the feel-good vibes of initial Stay Interviews carry over to that "no sign she's leaving" feeling. As a result, it's common for a company with 40 percent annual turnover to erroneously report 80 percent of their employees are green—that they will stay for at least another year.

In reality, we expect some greens will leave even if they cannot predict so themselves because lifestyle changes happen. But, ideally, we want to retain all the greens and move the acceptable-performing yellows and reds to green as well.

There are many models in the marketplace that predict which employees will leave based on selected variables. I recall one HR executive in China telling me that he connects on LinkedIn with all of his employees specifically so he can see when they are improving their profiles, which he read as an intention to leave. But while these models strive for accuracy, they tend to come up short on effectiveness because they produce data with no solutions. We ask our client managers on all levels to commit to a forecast that by itself deepens their commitment to retaining that employee. Those managers then become accountable for retaining the greens, which is their top priority, followed by retaining the yellows and reds if their performance merits so.

Forecasting plays one additional but essential role in our helping client organizations reduce their turnover. We meet with all supervisors on all levels in groups after they have completed their initial round of Stay Interviews to identify further retention actions, and we begin this meeting by displaying a pie chart of the overall green/yellow/red distribution. The ensuing discussion covers their beliefs for why so many employees are green, but, more pointedly, we ask that they describe the detailed situations for every yellow and red, minus employee names of course. As a group we then explore what actions are required to ultimately move those employees to green. This is where retention happens.

Component #5: Accountability

Ahh. We've saved the most powerful component for last. You might recall this italicized sentence from the beginning of this chapter: *The single greatest reason why organizations cannot reduce employee turnover is because they either hold the wrong people accountable for it or they hold no one accountable for it at all.*

Winding back to my initial foray into the retention space when I was working at the bank (see Chapter 2), this was our solution then: *You have a retention goal, go meet it, we'll be watching.*

The Finnegan's Arrow model, however, provides both goals and tools, all wrapped in metrics with a resulting culture of accountability. And all are completely aligned with the smartest research regarding reducing employee turnover. Note that the accountability component on the far right is then joined via sub-arrows underneath to goals and forecasts, the two metrics that managers are accountable for . . . and it is purposeful that these are the same metrics that salespeople are accountable for, which enables the c-suite to more easily adopt these mainstays of accountability.

Accountability matters such that we ask each client company to name a "Retention Champion," a top-line operations leader who brings authority to hold leaders accountable for not just making their goals but also facilitating Stay Interviews on time. This again moves employee retention accountability from HR or "everyone" to the top operations side of the organization—where this accountability has always belonged.

But for many organizations and the jobs within them, supervisors should not stand alone as being retention accountable. In manufacturing, for example, we are confident that achieving the new-hire goal will take us a long way if not completely to achieving our annual retention goal. In many cases, HR recruiters are essential contributors to our goal achievement because they decide who gets in the door, whether they are final deciders or just recommenders of who should be hired. Because these HR recruiters are the gatekeepers, they therefore must share accountability for achieving the new-hire goal. The same is true for designated new-hire trainers.

For client organizations with large numbers of new-hire recruiters, we find there is an immediate new-hire-turnover reduction by horse-racing those recruiters against each other, such that they can readily see the percentage of new hires whom they have permitted through the gate who have stayed throughout the new-hire goal period.

For tracking, we offer software that pulls data from each company's HR information system while also enabling each manager to input Stay Interview results, specific stay plans, and retention forecasts. Managers also input the top three reasons why each employee stays or might leave, which is more reliable than any engagement survey, and all of these data are ideal for driving retention accountability.

Combining Stay Interviews + Retention Accountability into Action

American Packaging Corporation reduced employee turnover during the Great Resignation and beyond via a strict diet of Stay Interviews and monthly manager retention accountability sessions, all while continuing other internal retention initiatives. With 1,300 employees across six plants, turnover has fallen since 2022 by a full 53 percent. Their executives tell us the most important initiatives for this improvement have been "listening to the voice of the employee," plus of course retention accountability.

More company success stories are included in Part Two.

A Concluding Accountability Idea

During our initial goal-setting session with executives, we often conclude by asking this seemingly innocent question: *How important is it that you achieve your two employee retention goals?*

As you can imagine, most initial answers are in the category of "very important." We push through to ask how important retention is *really*, relative to other top goals. The resulting executive-level discussion rarely yields a number, such as "retention is our fourth highest-priority goal," but our final request is that they build in accountability systems that are on the same level as patient care in hospitals, production goals in manufacturing, and other high-level metrics depending on their industry.

These examples represent top-five measurable goal categories and our recommendation is that they add achieving retention goals to these lists, even if they must bump a previously important goal category down to number six. And doing so requires the same level of follow-up and coaching diligence.

Retention accountability is rarely about removing a supervisor who struggles with continuing high turnover. Instead, we ask that our key metrics of retention performance against goal, Stay Interview completion, and forecast accuracy are discussed in team and individual leader meetings, just as our client companies do with their other important metrics.

A Summary of the Five Components of Finnegan's Arrow

1. Converting turnover to dollars so that executives fully grasp the immense cost of losing employees across a full year and take the proper actions to improve it.

2. Establishing retention goals for all turnover and for new-hire retention while specifying accountabilities for leaders on all levels as well as for HR recruiters and for new-hire trainers.

3. Training leaders on all levels to conduct Stay Interviews with their teams.

4. Asking leaders to forecast how long each employee will stay.

5. Developing reporting for accountability such that leaders become accountable for achieving their retention goals and for developing accurate forecasts.

5 ■ What Then Comprises a Trustworthy Boss?

Conscientious business followers know the troubled beginnings of Uber cofounder Travis Kalanick, made popular by the Showtime series *Super Pumped*.[1] That series and related reports present Kalanick as having been harassing, discriminatory, and rude, culminating in a video-gone-viral in which, after one of his own Uber drivers complained about decreasing pay rates, Kalanick said on dashcam video, "You know what? Some people don't like to take responsibility for their own s__t. They blame everything in their life on somebody else."[2]

This story is part of an in-depth *Harvard Business Review* report authored by two consultants who chose to help Kalanick heal his company's wounds. Their starting point was to help him build trust:

> We think of trust as precious, and yet it's the basis for almost everything we do as civilized people. Trust is the reason we're willing to exchange our hard-earned paychecks for goods and

services, pledge our lives to another person in marriage, cast a ballot for someone who will represent our interests.[3]

Warren Buffett is known to have said, "Trust is like the air we breathe—when it's present nobody really notices; when it's absent everybody notices."[4] Buffett was in fact echoing the groundbreaking psychologist Fredrick Herzberg. It was Herzberg back in 1959 who declared the difference between actions that motivate, such as recognition, and those that we quietly take for granted until they disappear, like trust.[5]

Buffett and Herzberg are both on my hero list, yet I'd look forward to debating either of them on whether employees take a trust-building supervisor for granted, as each of them imply. And the reason why today's employees so value a trusted supervisor is because most of us have lived on the other, darker side with a jerk boss who had little interest in trust or the how-to knowledge to ever build it. These are the supervisors who keep to themselves, grumble about their coworkers above and below them, and make no efforts to learn about their employees or share information about themselves. And the worst of them blame their turnover on pay and HR, understate their own impact, and mislead in other ways, thereby directing their teams by their own behaviors to skimp on their work and to ultimately quit.

The important point here is not only that workers leave jerk bosses but also that they stay for bosses who have developed trusting relationships with them. Trust-building supervisors are proactive drivers of employee retention, meaning employee retention is more than just the opposite of employee turnover. The supervisors in your company who successfully build trust with their teams have become intentional, proactive employee-retention drivers whose teams stay longer and whom others across your company crave to work for.

Supervisors have in fact been proven to have as much impact on an employee's mental health as that employee's spouse or partner.[6] This scientifically verified but out-of-left-field comparison underscores the importance of the very people you choose to manage your carefully selected employees—and to engage and keep them.

Trust's Place in Supervisory Training

Google "supervisory training" and you'll find traditional lists of curriculum topics like these:

- Employee recognition leads to employee motivation
- How to communicate more effectively as a new supervisor
- When to be flexible, and when to stand firm
- How to develop your own personal management style
- The truth about discipline—how to handle uncomfortable situations
- What every new supervisor and manager should know about hiring and firing
- Time management skills that really work
- Delegation, feedback, and communication
- Dos and don'ts of delegation
- Conversations, reviews, and conflict

I checked many vendors' training lists before finding the t-word. Yet the top business leaders who are mentioned above recognize trust as the most fundamental of all leadership qualities, and I learned the same long ago, during my academic training as a therapist and counselor. Social services academics have taught for decades that no leadership or helping relationship can be effective without first building a solid ground floor of trust.

Besides, could we realistically expect an employee to respond nicely to a supervisor's efforts to praise him or communicate with him if he didn't trust his supervisor in the first place?

Trust Matters More Today

Abraham Maslow's Hierarchy of Needs has remained a psychology staple since its inception in 1943. The model is represented as a simple pyramid that conceals the complexity of its original research.

Maslow's original hierarchy describes five levels of the human experience, with examples of how each need can be fulfilled. Each level must be sufficiently met before someone is prepared to tackle the next level. Here are the five levels, from the bottom up:

1. *Physiological*: water, food, shelter; the bare necessities for human survival
2. *Safety*: personal security, resources, source of income, structure, order
3. *Social*: friendship, intimacy, community, sense of belonging
4. *Esteem*: dignity, respect, achievement, purpose, recognition
5. *Self-Actualization*: creation, beauty, unity, aesthetics, exploration[7]

While Maslow theorized that humans progress from a lower level to the next higher level over time, it is also true that we can experience successes and lapses from one level to another, even during a single day.

For our trust discussion, let's focus on level two, safety. Three major social movements have impacted our personal sense of safety over the past several years, revealing that we can no longer take that sense of safety for granted:

- The #MeToo movement originated with people who were mostly women telling their sexual abuse stories over social media, before taking center stage with the convictions of Harvey Weinstein and other men of power. The movement alerted people of the world that sexual abuse was more prevalent and happened to a far broader group of victims than had ever been assumed before, including well-known celebrities.
- George Floyd's murder-by-cop was made real to the world by a video that displayed the full nine minutes and twenty-nine seconds that police officer Derek Chauvin drove his knee into Floyd's neck to asphyxiate him. One of many trust-breaking outcomes is that Black people and all people now have evidence that cannot be dismissed that an officer of the law actually did deliberately kill an innocent person who happened to be Black.
- And while "psychological safety" might be a new term to some, McKinsey's research has demonstrated not only that it is a driver of worker productivity but also that we have

too little of it. The term means "feeling safe to take interpersonal risks, to speak up, to disagree openly, to surface concerns without fear of negative repercussions or pressure to sugarcoat bad news." McKinsey's studies make clear that a psychologically safe environment improves retention, engagement, and more—yet too few managers have the skills and courage to create one.[8]

These are just three headliners among many social patterns that continue to evolve, all wrapped around the negative psychological swings that developed during the COVID-19 pandemic. The outcome is that people are seeking and welcoming relationships where they feel safe to be their authentic selves— both at home and in their places of work—and are much more willing to abandon relationships that feel insecure.

A Trust Recognition Exercise

When we train managers on how to facilitate Stay Interviews, we ask them to participate in the following exercise so the impact of a trustworthy supervisor versus an untrustworthy supervisor becomes personal to them:

1. Write the name or initials of the best boss you ever had.
2. Then do the same with the worst boss you ever had.
3. Now score your best boss on a scale of 1 to 10 regarding how much you trusted that supervisor.
4. And do the same with your worst boss, scoring how much you trusted that person on a scale of 1 to 10.
5. Now list the worst things your best boss did as a supervisor, their most obvious supervisory weaknesses.
6. And then list your worst boss's greatest strengths.

Then, with their fresh-thinking notes in front of them, we discuss the ease with which they can accept the shortcomings of a trusted leader versus the difficulty of seeing strengths in a leader they don't trust. And our conclusion is that how much an employee trusts his leader impacts his total perception of that relationship. In other words, those baseline perceptions of trust drive all other aspects of how we see that leader as a supervisor, including how they provide recognition, career coaching, and more.

Trust is the single go/no-go indicator in relationships, yet supervisory trainers lump trust in with approachability, communication, recognition, and feedback—as though trust has relationship peers. Trust has no peer for making relationships stronger or weaker.

How Should Supervisors Build Trust?

Let's begin by defining "supervisor" as anyone who manages people top-to-bottom on your organization chart, which includes the CEO.

In Chapter 3, I referred to the great work of Paul Zak, the Claremont Graduate University professor and neuroscience expert. By way of an elaborate chain of measurements conducted over more than fifteen years, Zak established that employees were more likely to facilitate collaboration, teamwork, and trust if they demonstrated increases in the brain chemical oxytocin.[9]

Zak ultimately identified eight supervisor behaviors that can increase their team's oxytocin levels and foster trust, which are summarized below:

- *Recognize excellence*, which has the largest effect on trust when it occurs immediately after a goal has been met, when it comes from peers, and when it's tangible, unexpected, personal, and public.
- *Induce "challenge stress"* by assigning difficult but achievable jobs and making employees work together in teams.
- *Give people discretion in how they do their work* but build in oversight and risk management procedures to ensure they operate within smart guardrails.
- *Enable job crafting* by allowing employees to choose which projects to work on when possible.

- *Share information broadly*, covering not just top-down company information but also daily communication between supervisors and direct reports.
- *Intentionally build relationships* because workers perform better when they care about each other and don't want to let their teammates down.
- *Facilitate whole-person growth*, including discussions about work–life integration, family, and time for recreation and reflection.
- *Show vulnerability*, for example by asking for help with a task where the supervisor is open about their own shortage of knowledge or talent.[10]

This list of trust-building behaviors is obviously easier to read than to actually perform. As with any other group of complex skills, supervisors must be trained to do these tasks and be measured on continual improvement. And the best way for them to learn is to model their supervisory styles after their own supervisors', who will hopefully perform their own jobs in these same ways. This skill list also provides guideposts for interviewing potential supervisors to measure their potential for trust-building success.

A Closing Thought

I've looked to many brilliant contributors in this chapter to underscore the importance of choosing and developing leaders who can lead their teams by building trust. Let's close with another message from Gallup chair Jim Clifton, here noting the importance of each manager you select:

> Here's something they'll probably never teach you in business school: The single biggest decision you make in your job—bigger than all the rest—is who you name manager. When you name the right people to manage your company's workplace, everything goes well. People love their jobs, your customers are engaged, and life is great. When you name the

wrong person manager, nothing fixes that bad decision. Not compensation, not benefits—nothing.[11]

Five Takeaways from This Discussion Regarding Supervisors and Trust

1. While supervisors who fail to build trust drive employees away, supervisors who do indeed build trust attract employees and retain them longer.
2. Trust is the bedrock human quality that is most required for strong interpersonal relationships.
3. Academics have long known this is true, so organizations must catch up by coaching leaders to build trust and holding them accountable for doing so.
4. The best way to open leaders' minds regarding trust's power is to facilitate them to examine their reactions to the various trust levels of their former leaders.
5. Those leaders who fail to build trust after coaching and training must be replaced by new leaders who can.

6 ▪ Trustworthy Bosses Facilitate Stay Interviews with Precision

They say there are just two kinds of meetings: *Did you do your work?* and *Here's more work.* But when facilitated correctly, Stay Interviews are a different kind of meeting.

This chapter is about how to make Stay Interviews work in your company and the detailed work required to implement them *with precision*. As has been true with all our client companies, we enter this discussion assuming that 90 percent or a nearby proportion of your first-line supervisors can and have already built trust with their teams. So, our focus will be on those winners who build skills to retain their teams versus the others who also learn and apply the Stay Interview. Their resulting goal-achievement data plus comparisons of exits to forecasts will shine light on how well they are succeeding.

And while Stay Interviews might sound like a soft approach to retention, they are bolstered via the Finnegan's Arrow model by data, making each leader accountable for achieving their retention goals and developing accurate forecasts. Stay Interviews would flounder without these guidepost metrics because some leaders would clearly see them as flavor-of-the-month and look forward to their going away. Yet Stay Interviews' value, and their power, eventually becomes clear.

Stay Interview Basics

A Stay Interview is a *structured* discussion a *supervisor* conducts with each individual employee to learn the specific actions he must take to strengthen that employee's engagement and retention with the organization

Structured means Stay Interviews have defined components that require comprehensive training for managers to facilitate them correctly—and that they are just one chunk of a larger process that improves engagement and retention. Stay Interviews are not "rounding" or "check-ins" that contain loose if any scripting along with no documentation or follow-up. Stay Interviews are sophisticated tools when applied correctly.

Supervisor refers to the direct-report managers who must conduct Stay Interviews with their individual team members. This group includes all who manage others, ideally from the CEO on down. Cascading in this way ensures that those supervisors who manage first-level workers enjoy their initial Stay Interview experience as an employee, which also reinforces the training they've experienced by watching their manager conduct their own Stay Interview in real time.

Stay Interviews must be conducted by first-line leaders for their teams and there can be no substitutes. Companies that assign the Stay Interview role to HR are depriving their managers of a trust-building experience, and the end product will be an employee wish list for even more one-size-fits-all programs.

A few companies have asked if using skip-level managers will cause employees to be more open. As Stay Interviews are exclusively a tool for first-line leaders only, those managers who cannot ultimately build trust with their teams must be replaced by other managers who can.

The Stay Interview Q5

A decade-plus of experience has proven that the Stay Interview Q5—the five original Stay Interview questions—still pack their full power today. Each question below fulfills one or more specific jobs, and all five then hang together to enable managers to learn all they need to retain and engage each individual employee better.

Q1: When you travel to work each day, what things do you look forward to?

This question fulfills two assignments, two jobs. Job #1 is directing the employee's thinking and her response toward day-to-day work, which is the area where most employees decide to stay or leave, and also the area where first-line supervisors have the most impact. Job #2 is converting the employee's mind from a negative outlook to a positive one.

As adults, we've been known to display a negativity bias that helps to "serve critical evolutionarily adaptive functions."[1] Or, said more clearly, our initial response to new stimuli is the same as if we were cave people with clubs, protecting ourselves from new dangers. Q1 brings the employee's mind into daily work with a smile. And we recognize that traveling to work today might be walking down a hall or climbing a flight of stairs.

Q2: What are you learning here? And what would you like to learn?

I used to see Q2 as "low-hanging fruit" until a manager corrected me by saying it actually produces fruit on the ground. Q2 pushes aside all discussions about career goals, career ladders, and other complex, long-term discussions that intimidate most managers. Instead, it assigns a very achievable assignment early in the interview that employees crave, and upon which managers can build trust. Besides, a high percentage of employees are not seeking careers in the traditional sense, and companies are likely to have legitimate career opportunities for some workers but not for all.

We train managers to ask for and also suggest training topics in order to identify at least one. And developing training solutions requires managers viewing every other employee on their campus as a potential teacher—as well as considering books, articles, the internet, and even YouTube. Managers can easily become individual employee training designers once they commit to identifying a subject, developing a training plan, and following up with the employee afterward to ensure that the training worked. And with repetition, managers become very comfortable doing this.

Q2 then is an early, stand-alone trust-builder that is based on fulfilling an identified and important individual employee need. And helping each employee learn new skills sends a clear message that the manager cares.

Q3: Why do you stay here?

Q3 is my personal favorite of the five, and has three different functions. First, once a manager knows the answers to Q1 and Q3—what the employee looks forward to and why they stay—*then they have just learned what makes the employee happy.* The manager can then design the employee's current and future jobs to include more of what they want. Second, by answering this question, each employee must now discover and announce to themselves why they stay, because most employees can't identify this immediately like they can when asked why they might leave—our brains are designed to be negative first. Finally, this positive question is asked immediately prior to asking the all-important negative question, Q4 (see below).

Many employees answer why they stay with "I have to pay the bills," which often is code for "I haven't really thought about it." We train managers to tell such employees that they could probably go elsewhere and make more money to more easily "pay the bills," and to say they are grateful they are staying. But managers should next probe deeply to ask why is it that employee *really* stays, and wait for a genuine answer rather than impatiently offer a multiple-choice probe like "Do you stay for the team? Or for our customers?"

This carefully trained method causes employees to then discover why they actually stay and announce it out loud in their own voices so their own ears can hear it, often for the very first time. So these employees have now disclosed to us and to themselves this crucial, not-always-known piece of retention information, all prior to their telling us why they might leave.

Q4: When was the last time you thought about leaving our team? What prompted it?

Q4 is deliberately direct, seeking the most important information during the Stay Interview session. It is positioned after the lead-up exchanges on what this employee looks most forward to, what they most want to learn, and why they stay, which act as the lubricant for an honest exchange.

How open the employee chooses to be depends in part on how the manager responds to each sentence. The manager's job here is to listen, record, and probe to clarify—not to solve or rebut. Employees are people, too, and people disclose more than they initially intend to when a listener expresses total interest in their words and disclosures by just listening alone. That single skill opens doors to sharing, and combined with probing and note-taking can lead to employees leaving the room having offered many more clues to retaining them than they anticipated sharing when they entered.

Q5: What can I do to make your experience at work better for you?

This final question can lead the employee to a general answer, so it is important for the manager to keep returning to "I." Probes such as "Do I tell you when you do something well?"; "Am I available when you need me?"; and "Do I communicate the right information on time?" will all blend together such that the employee will hopefully introduce those one or two things—or many more—that they wish their manager did differently.

And the best manager responses are to acknowledge understanding, thank the employee for feedback, commit to any willful changes, and clarify any critical misunderstandings.

Required Stay Interview Skills

"Don't do your own drywall" is code in our offices for leave the tough work to the pros, and Stay Interview training is best conducted by those who are highly skilled to do so. I describe below four specific Stay Interview skills. Managers who conduct Stay Interviews must be introduced to these skills by a very competent facilitator who includes skill-practice exercises so managers can practice conducting Stay Interviews during training before doing so with their teams.

Skill #1: Listening

Listening is voluntary whereas hearing is not. We hear every waking hour whether intentionally or via background chatter, but listening requires the Stay Interview manager to isolate focus on each employee. And that focus is both physical, meaning there are no other sounds or interruptions, and mental in that one's mind stays in the present tense. And, most importantly, the manager listens until the employee finishes speaking as opposed to already preparing what to say next. During Stay Interviews, listening is a mandated choice.

Great listeners know that some words matter more than others. The most important words are emotion words like *angry, frustrated, grateful,* or *overjoyed* because these words tell us the most important outcomes of the events being described. Let's role-play this concept:

> JUAN: I get so frustrated when Susan sits beside me every day but doesn't get her reports out. She's distracted on the phone, makes mistakes, interrupts me to ask the same questions over and over. Sometimes I get really angry with her.
> MANAGER: Hmm. I'll talk with Susan about this.

The manager here heard that Susan is an erratic-performing distraction for Juan but missed the two important emotion words *frustrated* and *angry*. A better response that indicates focused listening would be this:

MANAGER: Sheesh. I understand why you would get frustrated, Juan. And I would get angry sometimes, too. Let me address this with Susan, right away.

This response shares some emotion back, along with empathy and urgency, causing Juan to feel like his manager is listening deeply. Juan will likely share more information throughout the remaining Stay Interview discussion than he had planned to when he entered the room.

Skill #2: Taking Notes

Managers who scribble notes are indicating they are listening, leaning on every word. And they are documenting evidence for developing a resulting stay plan later that day or soon after the meeting. Imagine the value of two scribbled pages per employee with emotion words circled, arrows connecting one thought to another, and all done legibly enough so the manager can separate the most important thoughts of one employee from another.

There is evidence that scribbled notes bring more value than keyboard-entered notes because our brains retain written information longer.[2] Besides this, keyboards become physical obstacles between managers and employees, they can distract from eye contact, and perhaps most importantly they bring a sense of mystery into the room because employees can't see what their manager is inputting, whereas scribbled notes are out in the open.

Skill #3: Probing

Probing converts five Stay Interview questions into twenty questions or more. The combination of focused listening plus note-taking leads the manager to pick up cues for deeper investigation, and oftentimes the employee is deliberately leaving a breadcrumb path as a way to seek permission to tell more detailed stories. The best Stay Interview managers are the ones who identify these trails and probe their ways forward, chasing the breadcrumbs.

The two kinds of probes are *open* and *closed*. Open probes seek paragraphs of information such as "Tell me more," or "Can you give me an example?" Closed probes target one information chunk, for example asking for a name, a number, or a yes or no.

Both kinds of probes work in Stay Interviews because the manager's role is to gain enough information to learn why that employee stays, might leave, and what they can do to retain him.

Skill #4: Taking Responsibility

By nature of our Stay Interview questions, managers are actually inviting their employees to complain, so managers must be trained in how to respond to complaints. The obvious response skills are to avoid defensiveness, thank the employee for honest feedback, and consider if the shoe fits.

The greater danger, though, is when the employee invites the manager to co-complain by saying something like, "I see you roll your eyes when your boss walks away. You know we don't have enough staff or the right equipment to get our jobs done, yet you don't stand up for us to make things better." For this manager, the door just opened for him to "blame up," to say, "You know, I've tried, but I can't get support for you." And once this manager co-complains with his employee, once he becomes an accomplice, he demotes himself. He has now placed himself into a peer relationship with his employee, and that one moment of doing so will place a lifetime alteration on their manager–employee relationship.

The antidote line is this: *"Sure, I face some work challenges, too. But be assured that I'm all-in with our company, ten fingers and ten toes, and I intend to work here for a long time. But this is your meeting, so let's get back to your ideas about working here."*

Our now-prepared manager has practiced listening, taking notes, probing, and taking responsibility, and now has two or so pages of notes in order to build a stay plan.

Building Stay Plans

Stay plans are the resulting next-step actions based on each Stay Interview in which the manager has applied the four skills noted above. Managers now need to ask themselves the following question: *"Now that I've learned so much, what is it that I can fix?"* Managers who conduct Stay Interviews with precision unlock several subjects for discussion, and their resulting assignment is to identify the one or two most important subjects for action.

The temptation here is to imagine each employee requesting a 20 percent raise or a promotion for which she isn't qualified. Or for your company to redirect its strategic approach by developing new products. But the reality is that the great majority of things employees want are within their manager's scope. *They want their managers to address what they talk about over dinner.* The resulting stay plan might include just one or two sentences that describe what the manager will do, what the employee will do, and a closing date for each. By conducting the Stay Interview Q5, the manager now has detailed information on what that employee looks forward to each day, what they want to learn, why they stay, why they might leave, and how they want their manager to connect with them better.

Stay plans might contain one or multiple actions. Modifying a work schedule might be the best outcome for one employee, whereas another might want to learn a new skill. Yet another might want to be involved in a new project or even be introduced to another manager whose team does work they consider to be more appealing. The plan might be developed at the end of the Stay Interview session or a few days later.

One stay plan caution is to avoid shoehorning a complex issue into a simple response. Let's say an employee confides that he is overwhelmed by the volume and complexity of his work, that he feels like a bad spouse and parent because he works so much at home. The manager must patiently probe to learn more during the initial session or soon-scheduled future ones. But the worst response would be to wish this burdensome issue away by saying that this is the busy season, or that after we fill two openings, all will be better.

Most important is that the manager completes the assignments both sides agree on, all in order to build trust so that the employee attaches herself to her manager, further engages in her work, and stays.

Figure 8 provides seven common examples of how a manager could move forward from a specific topic introduced by an employee.

Employee Topic	Suggested Probes	Stay Plan Solutions
Communication	What specific information do you need? How can I best communicate it such as via email, in 1-1 meetings, in team meetings?	Solicit input for team meetings, schedule and don't postpone 1-1 meetings, communicate information more quickly, nominate employee for a specific-topic input group.
Conflicts with peers	When would you say was the first time you felt uncomfortable? What role might you have played in this conflict? What would you have done differently? What outcome do you want?	Coach employee to change behaviors. Bring employee together with others to resolve conflicts openly. If employee is a top performer, rearrange work relationships if necessary.
Development	If you could learn about just one additional topic related to your job, what would that topic be? How do you learn best? By observing? Practicing? Reading? When much lime do you need to team so we can schedule another meeting to review?	Ask an internal mentor to meet with the employee to teach the skills. Propose and agree on helpful books or websites. Recommend internal or external courses.
New role/ promotion	Tel me the perfect job for you. Why is that job so appealing to you? What skills do you have that qualify you for that job? What skills would you have to build?	Ask employee to shadow incumbent in desired job and report back on the five most important skills. Give employee feedback on her skill levels for the needed skills. Build a plan for the employee to develop skills via mentoring, coursework, and feedback.
Pay	How much money do you think you should be making? What actions do you see that you can take to increase your pay? What skills can you build that would make you more valuable to cur company?	Check employee's pay against same-performing peers to verify it is right. Design development plan that is targeted toward a higher-paying job if employee has talent to qualify. Ensure employee knows all incentive opportunities that would provide shorter-term rewards.
Recognition	Do you think being recognized would motivate you to perform even better? Tell me a time when you should have been recognized but were not. Would you rather be recognized privately or in front of others?	Commit to lending a sharper eye toward achievement that merits recognition. Ask employee to call your attention to achievements you might overlook. Nominate employee for company recognition awards if performance merits doing so.
Too Much Work	Which assignment gives you the most stress? What do you see as the three most important priorities and assignments in your job? What additional stalls can you build? What are you doing that is less necessary or can be done by others?	Reduce stress by lengthening timelines, building skills, or reassigning work. Eliminate unnecessary duties. Help employee learn new needed skills.

Figure 8: Suggested Probes and Stay Plan
Source: C-Suite Analytics and Richard P. Finnegan.

It then offers suggested probes the manager could say to draw out more information on the topic, followed by ideas that could be included in the resulting stay plan.

The following guidelines round out the Stay Interview process:

1. To start, managers top-down should conduct Stay Interviews with all employees and for new hires two times during the new-hire goal period, and then for all employees every six or twelve months after.

2. Managers should conduct their first Stay Interview with an employee with whom there is already mutual comfort in order to make the initial session easy.

3. Managers should ask the five Stay Interview questions precisely as they are written, rather than adjust them for their own preferences or comfort.

4. Despite the temptation, managers should never send the questions in advance lest they waste time responding to the employee's predetermined lists rather than discovering the most important topics together.

5. Importantly, managers should avoid any references to the employee's performance, focusing instead on the most glaring topics that ultimately connect back to that employee's engagement and retention.

Connecting the Dots from Chapter 1

Let's end this chapter by gluing together the data presented in Chapter 1 with the Stay Interview Q5, whose retention power has been proven across hundreds of companies for well over a decade.

First, many more employees are working from home or working hybrid schedules, and they will continue to do so because the overall talent shortage is giving employees so much power. Many employees in fact will report to a manager who they will never meet in person for the duration of their time with that employer. While companies are planning virtual happy hours and other superficial ways to build engagement and retention, Stay Interviews are a better answer because they provide a structured exchange that stimulates direct discussion and clear follow-up actions against the backdrop of leader accountability.

Second, young workers' needs and ambitions are much more personalized and specialized than for earlier generations, such that long-held traditional assumptions about what employees want are no longer true. The simplified results of engagement surveys and exit surveys further build this false narrative. If we want to know what our employees want, we must ask them—and the "we" must be their direct supervisors.

And third, the Great Gully data presented in Chapter 1 indicates we are flat-out running out of workers, and many whom we hire will come via different languages and cultures. Stay Interviews have proven to be a top retention solution, and they enable us to keep the workers we want along with the chutzpah to terminate those we don't.

7 ■ Stay Interviews' Impact on Contemporary Employee Issues

Our emerging but limited workforce will always bring new issues with them. While many of these will relate to societal norms and demographics, individual employees will also bring their own unique experiences and perspectives. This introductory sentence will become cellophane clear as this chapter unfolds.

Four Steps to Improve Millennial and Gen Z Retention
Often considered to be youngsters, these two generational groups together comprise more than half of our current workforce. And that percentage increases every day. Below are four steps to improve your retention of millennial and Gen Z employees.

Step #1: Lock in on These Key Employee Retention Words: Flexibility, Mobility, Entrepreneurial Freedom
Maybe we should develop an acronym for those words so we can say them more quickly. Let's settle on "MEFF" for today.

Microsoft says these are the at-work values young workers hold onto most dearly. Their study covered thirty-one thousand workers across thirty-one countries, along with analysis of "trillions of productivity signals in Microsoft 365 and labor trends on LinkedIn."[1] Any study that references trillions makes me buy in. One employee quote from the Microsoft study nails how the pandemic changed the ways our workforce reconsidered their jobs: *"Covid has not been all doom and gloom for me. It forced me to dig deep and reevaluate what is important."*

Step #2: Consider Your Company's Opportunities to Provide MEFF for Employee Retention

Words like "boundaries" help our minds build fences whereas words like "opportunities" knock those fences down. Way back before the pandemic made working from home a hip thing—that's "dope" for my young readers—I read a study that rank-ordered jobs that could be done remotely. Technology workers sat atop the list, with teachers at the bottom.

Let's split your jobs into two categories, with Group A being those jobs where MEFF is imaginable (e.g., financial analysts) and Group B where MEFF seems impossible (e.g., nurses, security guards, manufacturing workers, bartenders)—the jobs where employees must be in the same location every day.

If your company is comprised mainly of Group A jobs, the so-called knowledge workers, you have an easier path. Your main challenges are to wake up your executive team with publications like this one so they open their minds to MEFF and then update policies so that employees can contribute on their own schedules and from wherever.

Step #3: Rethink How MEFF Employee Retention Meshes with Work Schedules

Rereading our MEFF words tells us *mobility* is out for Group B jobs, so *flexibility* must be in. Here are six ways to increase schedule flexibility:

1. Lock in scheduled workdays and hours with as much advance notice as possible so employees can plan their nonwork hours around families, schools, and other life events.

2. Forced shift rotations must end for the sake of employees' mental and physical health and so they can schedule school and other priorities while also getting adequate and consistent sleep.

3. Pay employees to accommodate their peers by changing shifts for a day. Commit to paying any coworker who says "yes" an additional three dollars an hour for the shift they take. That's buying increased flexibility for about $25 per schedule change, which is peanuts compared to the cost of losing high-performing employees.

4. Honor those employees who volunteer to change schedules most frequently. Post how often they say "yes" publicly, so all know they are schedule-changing heroes. Hold quarterly shift-change hero drawings for gift cards or weekend getaways where each shift change equates to one slip of paper in the bowl. Give shift-changers extra credit for their unique contributions because you must retain them.

5. Base all permanent shift changes on performance versus length of service, otherwise you are telling sharp new hires they will be long stuck on a shift they don't prefer so they'll eventually quit.

6. Significantly increase shift differentials. Per-hour pay means more to those seeking work than those already onboard. Signify to potential new hires that you will make it worthwhile for them to adjust their lives to meet your business needs.

Step #4: Train Your Leaders to Conduct Stay Interviews for Employee Retention

Steps 1–3 assume all employees want the same things, but in reality they do not. Retention is now an individualized game, and your best retention solution continues to be each employee's direct supervisor. This is the person whose name your employees say over dinner, surrounded by good adjectives or bad. Let those supervisors learn how best to retain each member of their teams and then hold them accountable for doing so.

Not all MEFF-related issues can be solved by policies alone. Supervisors conducting Stay Interviews are your best opportunity to identify the *entrepreneurial freedom* in MEFF. Train supervisors to listen—truly listen—to what each employee needs to thrive and to stay. Together with their manager, they can find one-off assignments, task force participations, and even readings and webcasts for employees to grow new skills.

Fairness in the Workplace Will Always Matter

Terms like "equal opportunity," "affirmative action," and "diversity" have had long and sometimes contentious lifespans in our business lexicon. But their anchoring value is *fairness*, which is something we all believe in, and which is bolstered by that phrase in the Declaration of Independence that we learn in school: "All men are created equal", which would eventually include women as well.

A recent Monster survey underscored this importance as a full 91 percent of respondents said they had personally experienced discrimination related to race, gender, disability, age, or body size.[2] So it's clear that unfairness—or the perception of it—continues throughout our workplaces.

Moving past this "nearly all of us have felt this way" data outcome, my gut response is a practical one: No employer can afford to push away talent when talent is in such short supply. But a deeper dive reveals that organizational efforts at fairness have ranged from what some would call quotas to various one-size-fits-all programs such as minority-specific recruiting, diversity directors and departments, and affinity groups.

What's the crucial missing piece? *Supervisor–employee relationships.* Knowing now that 70 percent of employee engagement hinges on these relationships, that employees' opinions of their bosses drive their opinions of their pay, benefits, development, and advancement . . . and that the number one reason employees stay or leave or engage or disengage is how much they trust their boss, then we would all agree that overlooking this absolutely most important component in currently found approaches for workplace fairness is an essential missing link.

Given that all fairness feelings begin with the supervisor–employee relationship, the five Stay Interview questions then become the pivot points for leaders to learn how to retain and engage each individual employee. And the resulting conversations become natural and free-flowing, generating the required levels of openness where sensitive issues can be introduced and addressed.

Retaining Black Workers in Particular

While fairness initiatives benefit all of us, new data have emerged regarding how Black workers feel as part of the American workforce. The following data from McKinsey relates to the progress patterns of over *four million employees*:

- Half of Black workers say they receive little or no support to advance their careers, more than the 40 percent who say the same from all other racial groups.
- Just 29 percent of Black employees believe promotions are merit based.
- Forty-eight percent of Blacks believe their race alone makes it harder to achieve their promotion goals, nearly twice as many for other minority groups. Or, said another way, about half of all Black employees begin work each day believing the promotion game is not fair for them based on the color of their skin.[3]

And here's a stunner: *McKinsey researchers calculated it would take nearly a century for every level of the corporate pyramid to mirror the Black share of the total population.* "But by tackling key barriers such as higher attrition and lower odds for career advancement among Black workers, companies could reach that milestone in 25 years."

That number of years is stated optimistically, telling us just how far behind we are.

All of these data make clear that employee retention and engagement among our nation's Black employees is a very long way from acceptable.

The report goes on to describe current "solutions," including anti-bias training for managers, requiring "racially diverse slates" for promotion consideration, and diverse hiring panels. Some companies are establishing hiring and promotion goals, reflecting back to the era when HR professionals were more fearful of federal government compliance enforcement.

Each of these ideas represents true good-faith efforts but are obviously not enough. What is missing here again is holding supervisors accountable for developing and retaining their teams, including their Black employees. Assuming every Black employee is going to work each day with the identical concerns about work is no more valid than assuming white employees do the same. Productive, two-way communication about needs and worries happens best between employees and their supervisors, and for those employees their supervisor is the one person—the *only* person—who learns their strengths and their interests each day.

My mind races toward what we refer to here as Q2, the second Stay Interview question, which is "What are you learning here?" We train leaders on all levels to ask this question regardless of whether their employee is in his fifth week or fifth year, acknowledging responses will be different. A new hire will tell you what they've learned and where the gaps are for them to excel in their new jobs. A veteran employee might say, "I'm learning nothing and just want to do my job and go home," which is very OK. But another veteran employee might say, "I'm bored" or "I want to learn this skill" or "I want to advance to this job."

My additions to the solutions included in the McKinsey study would include the following:

1. Train all leaders, everywhere, to conduct Stay Interviews, so those leaders can both build trust with their individual

Black employees and also learn what is important to them, both for retention and engagement.

2. Include in that Stay Interview training role-plays for how to manage each employee's response to Q2, "What are you learning here?" This role-play training is standard for each Stay Interview program we teach for client companies.

3. Hold those leaders accountable to goals for both retaining and engaging their teams, including every employee on their teams.

No trendy new program that is designated specifically for an employee group will ever have as much influence on each employee as will their immediate supervisor.

If You Need Another Reason to Do Stay Interviews, #MeToo Is It

I can tell you scores of reasons why Stay Interviews are right for you and your company, long before crossing the waters toward the #MeToo movement, which is loaded with controversy. But now is the time to muscle directly toward that controversy.

All employees, not just women, need their forum to announce abuse. Abuse comes in many forms, with sexual harassment being just one example. Bullying fits in this category, as does any action that pits someone with power against another.

I've worked in organizations and know firsthand that such abuse sometimes happens at the supervisor level and also at higher levels, too. Sexually harassed employees tend to like their jobs, want to keep their jobs, but learn through very bad circumstances they must accede to weird, uncomfortable demands to keep their jobs. Those demands at the extreme are about sexual activities, but sometimes they are just about taking undeserved abuse from someone whose power exceeds theirs or doing something illegal or unethical because they are told to do so.

Of course, peers and nonmanagerial employees sometimes try to take advantage of their working colleagues, too, by leveraging various forms of authority or just employing a strong personality to coerce or intimidate. Consider this example: A woman is sexually harassed and, wanting to keep her job, looks for the best way to avoid confrontation. An uninformed outsider would say, "Why didn't she just say no?" The answer is she had bills to pay, likes her day-to-day job otherwise, and is seeking ways to survive.

Stay Interviews open the door to communication. Some supervisors are in the dark regarding managers above them who are making sexual-favor-innuendoes to members of their teams, or about others doing the same from any corner of their companies. The supervisors themselves might be the actual perpetrators and will need to be directly confronted.

Further, some supervisors are unaware of others' perceptions of their own behaviors, not realizing that a comment that seems natural to them might be offensive to others. Imagine this scenario where a supervisor asks an employee, "When was the last time you thought about leaving? What prompted it?" and the employee says, "You are the reason. It's OK if you tell me I look nice, but it's not OK if you tell me I look nice in a tight sweater."

These are the conversations that need to happen. Employees must be invited to confront sexual harassment, and for that matter any type of abuse. Even more so if that harassment is happening at a higher level.

There is no perfect fix for eliminating such abuse. Stay Interviews, however, open another door of communication, one that is not tied to performance or any type of coaching session. Requiring your managers to introduce Stay Interviews provides each organization with a better, more informed way to open up conversations with their employees and brings abuse of any kind into the open.

Retaining Workers in Poverty and Reducing Their Absences

I grew up in a run-down neighborhood on the north side of Pittsburgh, one that will never, ever, be accused of gentrification. We were officially the lower middle class, and my wonderful parents made sure we had all we needed but little else. I never knew what we didn't have because kids only know their immediate surroundings.

But this wasn't poverty. In their book *Bridges Out of Poverty*, Ruby K. Payne, Philip DeVol, and Terie Dreussi-Smith define poverty as *"the extent to which an individual does without resources."*[4] They then list nine categories of resources that go way beyond money: financial, emotional, mental, spiritual, physical, support systems, relationships/role models, knowledge of hidden rules, and coping strategies.

I kept searching for clues as to how a poverty-stricken person views work, clinging to the naïve notion that work = money = getting out of poverty. According to this equation, one would give all to their job as the ticket out. Then I read this:

> Like many individuals who live in poverty, Sally doesn't know the middle-class rules about not missing work or being late. She has brought her poverty-culture rules to work. They include relying on others to cover her workload while she takes care of her kids. The supervisor, operating from a middle-class orientation, is baffled by Sally's chaotic lifestyle, a boyfriend whom Sally cannot rely upon, and the failure of Sally to find some consistent way to solve her childcare needs. Sally has held a number of jobs, not the quality of this one. She never kept any of them for very long.[5]

A big lesson for me is that a poverty-stricken person's reality is worse than I thought, in this example due to Sally's *lack of support systems and ignorance of "the middle-class rules."*

Our hearts hurt people like Sally, yet our job requirements usually call more for rules than heart. While we cannot improve the lives of every Sally who comes looking for a job, we must recognize the only behaviors we can change are our own. How can we do a better job of hiring and retaining poverty-stricken applicants like Sally?

Here are a few ideas, starting with pre-hire:

1. Make your attendance and tardiness policies as clear as possible; say them, hand them out in writing, state how many employees you have terminated in recent months because of these policies.

2. Tell a story about an ex-employee who tried but failed to meet these policies due to complex life issues, withholding the employee's name but providing as many details as you can.

3. Make clear the procedure for notifying if one will be absent or late, saying that notification is required versus being a no-call, no-show.

4. Ask if the candidate has transportation for work and follow up on specifics she offers to ask if those methods are reliable.

5. Ask the candidate's confidence on a scale of 1 to 10 that he can achieve your attendance/tardiness policies for the first ninety days; ask him to remove himself from your applicant pool if he has any doubts he can get to work according to your requirements.

Then, after hire, coach newly hired employees who miss work as you can now ask more detailed questions. With very supportive words and tones, ask about back-up childcare, back-up transportation, and probe for other problems that cause employees to miss work or show up late. Help them identify solutions they might not have discovered on their own. Leverage the power of Stay Interviews and their designated high-focus time to dig deeply for causes and solutions.

None of these ideas guarantee your new hire will consistently show up, but this last idea might help the most: *Change your exit reason for new hires who violated your attendance policy from "attendance" to "attendance/bad hire."*

Changing "attendance" to "attendance/bad hire" makes clear that whoever was involved in the hiring decision took a bad risk. We should expect HR recruiters to screen for attendance with more detail than hiring managers, though some hiring managers might actually do it better. Regardless, those who take risks based on a candidate's past employment trends or answers to the pre-hire interview questions are likely to think harder and decide better when they know they are accountable for the outcome.

Can Stay Interviews Solve the US Military's Turnover?

Most of us have never considered the US military having turnover problems. Some time ago, I was approached in a book-signing line by a military "retention specialist," sent to hear me speak by his commanding officer, and from there our meetings began. Your initial thoughts might match mine, which were how can enlisted soldiers quit, and what variables are there among them? Aren't they all treated exactly the same with pay, benefits, and opportunities?

Several meetings later, a fascinating trend emerged. The reenlistment rate correlated with how much each soldier trusted their commanding officer. Those who built solid, productive, caring relationships led more soldiers to reenlist, while those who looked more like the commanding officers we see in movies—the tough kind—had far fewer soldiers choose to do so.

This comes as no surprise, as we now know that first-line leaders who build trust increase their odds of retaining those employees they want to keep, and that those who fail to build trust are rolling the dice. And I am confident soldiers refer to their substandard leaders as "jerk bosses" or worse, just like your employees do.

Three Closing Messages Regarding Contemporary Employee Issues

1. Stay Interviews and supervisors building one-to-one trust are essential components in all retention scenarios, as demonstrated by the wide range of examples presented here.
2. Reading these examples provides even more evidence that one-size-fits-all programs—which are used by most companies—have limited impact on retention.
3. People are individuals first, bringing their own unique genes, histories, skills, and preferences, so retention fixes must be customized to their own life stories.

8 ■ Hiring Workers Who Stay

Organizations typically use hiring tools to identify the best candidates such as structured interviews or various assessments that most of us refer to as tests. Whichever methods they use, their main objective is to measure whether someone *can* do the job. The second and far less applied objective is to measure whether that candidate *will* do the job. What is completely missing from most organizations' array of selection tools is whether they can measure through their hiring process *how long that employee will stay.*

Employers tend to think they can measure how long someone will stay based on how long they stayed in their past jobs. But the impact of the COVID-19 pandemic followed by the Great Resignation's flurry of job switching has both clouded this metric and provided many good-faith or not-so-good-faith reasons for quitting. Below I present four ways to hire employees who will stay that most companies don't apply.

1. Develop Realistic Job Previews

Realistic job previews (RJPs) are magic for screening out bad potential hires or for causing wrong candidates to withdraw. Our work
with clients tells us that RJPs help to reduce early turnover.

The best method is to identify the top three reasons employees in
the same job quit or get fired, and then communicate them not only
clearly but *sensorially* by "smacking" the candidate's senses. If the production floor gets hot, take them to the heat. If the job requires
travel, show them a typical monthly schedule. If nurses must work
holidays, hand them their likely holiday season assignments, including Christmas Eve.

My favorite RJP we developed was for a national fast-food company where we got permission for managers to take candidates
behind the counter. Station #1 was the griddle where employees
showed burn marks on their arms and the manager said, "Your hair
will smell like onions for as long as you work here." Station #7 was
the public restrooms where the manager displayed a seven-page
detailed instruction manual that included scrubbing the base of
the toilet and the corners. Then, to emphasize accountability, the
manager told the candidate that the district manager made unsched-
uled visits each week and would inspect the restrooms for cleanli-
ness. They would then check the cleaning sign-in sheet on the back
of the door to learn the name of the employee who did or did not
clean the restroom according to standards.

Another favorite was for a client who hired employees to work in
a cleanroom that mandated wearing the equivalent of a hazmat suit.
Using the restroom required removing the suit first and then show-
ering after, all prior to redonning the suit to return to work. So we
suggested each candidate put the suit on and walk up and down 150
feet of hallway to fully embrace this one example of their potential
working conditions.

One recent study tells us nearly 40 percent of hiring managers ad-
mit to lying to candidates about the role, its responsibilities, and its
potential advancement opportunities.[1] And who can blame them?
We've been taught to sell the job to the candidates we want, especially

in these times of dwindling numbers of attractive applicants. But once those candidates become employees, they experience the truth and also hear it from their peers, leading to early turnover and the obvious outcome of breaking trust.

It makes sense that the top reason for early quitting is getting first-week negative surprises on the job, and hardly anyone who quits your company in the first sixty days is quitting solely because of pay. Consider these topics that hiring managers might stretch the truth on or avoid discussing altogether:

- Pay, initially and ongoing
- Promotion opportunities
- Schedules
- Overtime
- Travel
- Outside-work weather conditions
- Inside-work heat or cold
- Specific duties of the job
- Redundancy of work
- Time required before changing shifts
- Potential of switching from part-time to full-time

RJPs should be followed by specific interview questions, starting with, "Everyone who takes our realistic job preview tour sees at least one part of our job they wish was different. What is that one part for you?" Deeper probing will alert both the manager and the candidate as to whether this job is the right fit, resulting in the manager making an offer or either party walking away.

2. Secure 50 Percent of New Hires from Employee Referrals

Your first thought as to why referrals stay longer and perform better—for which there is empirical evidence[2]—might be that current employees won't embarrass themselves by referring an unqualified candidate who showers infrequently. But a second reason might matter more: that referrals already know the ins and outs of your job because they've heard the downsides from their buddy and still find the job to be OK.

Most companies have referral programs but manage them in passive ways, relying instead on "post & pray" with various online recruiting companies to send them candidates. But now knowing that referrals are gold mines for talent because they do indeed stay longer and perform better requires us to switch to very active ways of managing them. Here are six outside-the-box ways to make your employee referral program perform more effectively, to fast-forward it to become a main piece of your total retention strategy:

1. *Establish a new-hire referral goal.* Continuously update it until at least 50 percent of your new hires come via referrals, consistent with an overall goal-driven retention approach.

2. *Assign one person to be accountable for achieving this goal.* Rotate the responsibility to inspire creativity, knowing that one person being accountable drives success better than everyone being accountable.

3. *Leverage your cost of turnover.* Calculating this value might cause you to double or even triple your current payout award.

4. *Pay 100 percent of the dollar award you choose to pay on the first day the referred employee reports to work.* The common habit is to pay some percentage of the award on day one, let's say 50 percent, and the rest later as though the referring employee is responsible for seeing that their referral stays for a few months and doesn't quit early. Referring employees are not responsible for employee retention, and the notion that they should be penalized if your management team makes a poor hiring decision or drives the referral away is obviously unfair. Money to be paid later doesn't motivate them, especially when a full 77 percent of American workers live paycheck to paycheck.[3]

5. *Double your award for life for employees who refer five successful new hires.* Feeding the horses is essential because a few employees are much more socially wired than others, and your cost of turnover will verify that nearly any reasonable referral award is a company bargain, even if you double it.

6. *Target new hires for referrals.* Newly hired employees just left a full team of workers, so they have plenty of recent contacts to refer—plus they want to make a good first impression.

One client company has connected the dots between the cost of turnover and referral awards in a fresh-thinking way. The company provides vehicle crash-repair services, with the key job being technician. Technicians were the certified workers doing the hands-on work of repairing the vehicles. They feature on the list of other skilled craftspeople whose numbers are decreasing throughout our country, which increases the challenge of replacing exits with equally skilled workers.

Company executives leveraged the initial turnover cost study by adding that the average technician brings in about $50,000 in revenue per month, which happens to be the same period most technician jobs stay open. Consequently, they simplified the numbers to provide current technicians with an impactful offer: *Anyone who successfully refers a new technician will earn an extra $2 for every hour the new technician works in their first year.*

The job offers much overtime such that the referring technician could earn up to an additional $5,000 for one successful referral. If the new technician works less than a full year, however, the referring technician would earn a lesser amount. While the company offered what some would consider a very high number of dollars per referral, they only did so after considering the full cost of losing and having to replace a technician.

3. Make Stay-Commitment Job Offers

There are but a handful of jobs for which we want to legally bind an employee to stay, but there is no law restricting us from asking for an ethical commitment from every new hire.

Imagine your managers saying this after delivering their standard job offer:

- "While I prefer you say 'yes' to my offer, I'd prefer even more if you refused my offer if you cannot see yourself staying with us for at least a full year."
- "So as you consider the next twelve months, please consider the likelihood that you might return to school, relocate, or accept a different job that you might have already applied for."
- "Or you might be iffy about the details of our job, or maybe the pay, or even working for me . . . although by extending this offer, I am all in on helping you succeed with our company."
- "Most importantly, our relationship will be based on trust and that starts now. So I'm hoping you will accept my offer, with the full ethical belief that you will stay with us for at least one year."

And if you want to add further strength, offer them an overnight to consider the offer and ask what time you should call them the next day.

There are two reasons for adding this commitment-infused offer. The first is obvious: Most employees will say "yes" only if they fully buy in to the requested one-year commitment. The second is that they will remember this commitment on the worst day of their first year, which will further influence them to stick it out and stay.

4. Assign Recruiters the New-Hire Retention Goal

In Chapter 4, I mentioned that HR recruiters should be held accountable for retention goals, and it's time now to dig into this idea more deeply.

In most companies, HR recruiters refer candidates to managers who then have the authority to make the hiring decision. A commonly said retention instruction is that managers must make retention-inspired hiring decisions because they are the ultimate deciders of who joins or does not join their companies. Fair enough.

The other perspective, though, is that HR recruiters should be very skilled at deciphering whether a candidate should be permitted to walk through the initial hiring gate and be interviewed by the hiring manager. They should also be able to determine whether the candidate *can do the job, will do the job*, and *will stay*. These recruiters open or close the door to each applicant, so they play an essential role in reducing employee turnover, especially new-hire turnover.

The best recruiters fully understand the competencies for the job as well as serving as an initial smell test for whether a candidate merits a look-see from the hiring manager. These best-in-class recruiters set up their managers to make solid hiring decisions by eliminating those applicants who don't merit a manager interview. All of this generates an easy argument that new-hire recruiters should share in and be tracked against their company's new-hire retention goal, measured by what percentage of candidates they pass on who are eventually hired and who remain with their companies during the new-hire goal period.

New-hire recruiters might counter that they have no influence post-hire regarding how the hiring manager treats that employee or any other factor in their post-hire employment. This is also fair enough. But those recruiters will make more informed decisions on whom they pass on for a manager interview once they see reports indicating they are being tracked against their company's new-hire goal. And comparing their performance against that of multiple recruiters creates an impactful new-hire retention competition, which is better than fair enough.

Four Smart but Rarely Fully Utilized Methods for Hiring Employees Who Stay

1. Develop realistic job previews for high-turnover jobs so new hires stay longer, such that you exceed your new-hire retention goal.

2. Proactively juice your employee referral program such that at least 50 percent of new hires come from referrals.

3. Train managers to deliver job offers in a way that generates an ethical stay commitment.

4. Hold internal recruiters accountable for achieving your new-hire retention goal.

9 ■ 3 Best-Practice Turkeys + 1 Wise-Owl Idea

Throughout these pages, I've presented much data to prove which solutions are real ones for reducing employee turnover and which are fakes—poor substitutes for what actually works. Let's explore three of the latter that consume much money and energy only to fail, along with a good one that has been hidden under wraps for decades.

Turkey #1: Employee Exit Surveys

If five is the maximum number of turkey icons we would use as a rating metric, exit surveys would win all of those gobblers. The often-applied medical metaphor is that exit surveys are autopsies, meaning they provide the real reasons employees quit so management can fix those reasons, and turnover then falls. But to keep up the medical analogy, let's call exit surveys toe tags instead.

Too harsh? Many times I've polled HR audiences on their use of exit surveys by asking these two probes:

1. *Please raise your hand if your company does employee exit surveys in any form.* Almost everyone raises their hands.
2. *Now please raise your hand again if you can think of one good outcome for your company as a result of your conducting exit surveys.* Less than 5 percent raise their hands.

On the surface, exit surveys should become strong tools to improve employee retention if they meet the following conditions:

- The survey is designed to elicit the real reasons employees leave.
- The employee tells the truth.
- The organization addresses the newly discovered leave reasons by solving the problems at their roots.

But none of those things happen, and here's why.

"Better Opportunity"

Some time ago I went on a Google quest to learn the supposed number one reason employees quit their jobs, and *better opportunity* was the winner. It's the winner because nearly every exit interview questionnaire contains this response, whether the questionnaire is delivered by a person, by an online program, or by a third-person interviewer.

Since we associate opportunity with pay or career, the resulting assumption is that some other company swooped in and made our employee an offer, and that offer was financially enticing or was for an exciting, higher-level job. There's absolutely nothing we could have done to stop that. Especially the assumed much-higher-pay part.

The truth is that "better opportunity" could have also meant a shorter commute, working with nicer people, or abandoning a jerk boss. Accepting that phrase as a leave reason is mush.

But the greater point beyond "better opportunity" being misleading is that it also implies that a new job just appeared. And those who are leaving an employer know this is a safe answer because any short explanation that they provide for accepting their "better opportunity" ends the discussion.

The outcome is that "better opportunity" avoids the more deeply rooted, drill-down discussions that come from asking questions like *"Why did you look?"*

Most job changes today require the job-changer to go online and click. That first click is the first step toward changing jobs. For a very select few, this first step is instead a direct inquiry from another company pitching a job that your employee didn't know was available and had never considered. But for the great majority of job-changers, the first step is that proactive click. So much better exit interview questions are:

- When did you initiate your job search?
- Why did you initially decide to leave us?
- Was there one trigger event that caused you to seek out other jobs?
- What's the single-best thing we could have done to keep you?

The one overlap between exit interviews and Stay Interviews is that qualified interviewers must bring great probing skills. They must recognize which broad responses contain juicy behind-the-scenes details that lead to solutions and then probe their way down that cookie-crumb trail to learn deep-seated truths. They must do all this regardless of whether that interview's objective is to learn why an employee is leaving or how to better help an employee to stay.

Conducting exit interviews in a way that will actually help your company is not, let's say, an entry-level job, but instead one that requires training, practice, and feedback on how effectively that exit interviewer can seek out the real reason each employee has chosen to look and then to leave.

Minimal Truth-Telling

While the above section addresses a common exit survey design flaw, employees still have little reason to "speak their truth," especially when inputting data into a computer or talking to a stranger.

Let's make a safe assumption here that employees' greatest frustration with employee engagement surveys—*"I told you, and you didn't address my complaint"*—applies to employee exit surveys as well. Then why would an employee who has already checked out of her job believe that retelling her story will make things better, for her or the person who replaces her? Besides, she's already told her story to a few work peers and outside friends, and she's ready to move on with her life.

Exit survey design flaws combined with many employees' reluctancy to be open make for an easy way out. If they can get by with "better opportunity" or by clicking just a few keys during an online survey, then telling abbreviated stories or misleading ones becomes easy and OK.

Provide Real Solutions

In most companies, exit survey results are tabulated into a report that is delivered upstream monthly or quarterly, depending on turnover volume. That report rank orders the reasons employees leave, often placing "better opportunity," "pay," or "career" at the top. Next steps are usually to build a few one-size-fits-all programs or do nothing at all.

The reality, however, is that the number one reason employees stay or leave is how much they trust their managers, and rarely are exit survey results delivered to that employee's supervisor. And if they are, the results are left to that supervisor to read, interpret, and decide what, if any, future changes he should make to his supervision style, with little or no coaching coming from above.

While exit surveys bring a concept that at first glance should be helpful to our overall retention quest, the combination of poor survey design, minimal truth-telling, and the absence of constructive follow-up dilutes their value.

The Best Exit Solution I Know

Years ago, I was speaking at the Chicago University Club to about a hundred senior managers who were attending a conference there. The topic of exit surveys came up, and after extensive group discussion a man in the back right corner raised his arm, stood up, and spoke with great wisdom.

This man explained that he was CEO of a four-hundred-employee consulting firm in Portland, Oregon, and that he needed every one of his talented and cherished employees for his firm to successfully win over and retain top clients. Accordingly, when an employee quit, he applied a protocol that was widely known throughout his management ranks. No rehire could begin until he as CEO signed the new-hire requisition order, and his managers understood he wouldn't sign that order until they had scheduled an in-person meeting with him to discuss why that employee had left and what that manager could have done to retain the employee.

This CEO's method worked because (1) he was skilled such that he would ask tough questions regarding why each employee left; (2) he was immediately following up at the likely root cause; and (3) his managers knew that any exit led to an uncomfortable interaction with the CEO, so they were motivated to build trusting relationships with each employee in order to keep them.

Turkey #2: Employee Engagement Surveys

If employee exit surveys merit five turkeys, let's assign employee engagement surveys just four of those guys.

Gallup tells us that employee disengagement costs US companies $8.8 trillion each year, which would certainly justify companies conducting annual engagement surveys—if they addressed this costly problem.[1]

The most glaring shortcoming with engagement surveys isn't that employees don't tell the truth, nor that in many companies that survey participation is low, nor even that most companies' survey results remain stagnant year after year—even though for many companies all of the above are true. *The massive swing-and-miss here is the inevitable onslaught of one-size-fits-all programs, coupled with the complete absence of any first-line manager accountability.*

Here's the typical company-wide drill:

1. Employees are invited to participate in their company's employee engagement survey electronically by a given date.
2. Management receives results about a month after that date.
3. HR leads the top team through a results discussion, maybe including benchmark data from similar companies.
4. HR is assigned to develop a survey-improvement plan.
5. Managers on whatever level for which the survey provides data are given the same assignment for their departments.
6. The CEO sends a carefully crafted email to all employees regarding survey results and a summary of action steps.

And then this same company surveys again a year or two later, seeing little change in results.

Like our tongues drifting over and over toward a recently chipped tooth, companies cannot help themselves from believing that employees stay or leave, or engage or disengage, based on whether those employees participate in company-wide, one-size-fits-all programs. We now know that the true fix is developing individualized, one-on-one relationships that each supervisor initiates with each member of his team.

William Kahn is the Boston University professor who in 1990 first used employee surveys to measure how engaged employees were in their jobs.[2] Gallup subsequently became the employee engagement giant by doing extensive product development and research on this topic, for both client and nonclient companies.

Since 2000, Gallup has produced annual reports of employee engagement levels by country, region, and globally, and these reports are considered to be supreme relative to any other data-driven employee engagement reports. Gallup groups US and Canadian data together, and Figure 9 shows their comparative analysis of employee engagement in these two countries over the past twenty-five years.[3]

Gallup's levels of engagement and their definitions are:

- *Engaged employees* work passionately and feel a profound connection to their company. They drive innovation and move the organization forward.

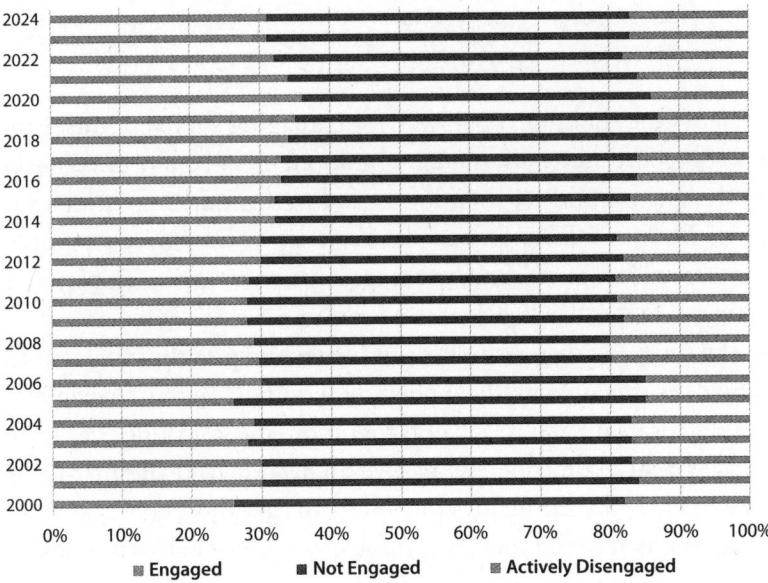

Figure 9: Gallup's Employee Engagement
Source: Gallup published data. Permission to reproduce.

- *Disengaged employees* are essentially "checked out." They're sleepwalking through their workday, putting time—but not energy or passion—into their work.
- *Actively disengaged employees* aren't just unhappy at work; they're busy acting out their unhappiness. Every day, these workers undermine what their engaged coworkers accomplish.

Figure 9 tells us that over a full twenty-five-year period there have been small gains and small losses, but overall there has been little positive movement at all. And Gallup recently announced that employee engagement had reached an eleven-year low.[4]

Gallup attributes this absence of engagement improvement to areas like lack of job clarity, a short supply of manager skills, or survey burnout among other reasons.[5] But here is the real reason:

Firstline managers are hardly, if ever, held accountable for increasing their employee engagement scores. Instead, the plethora of one-size-fits-all programs give employees "solutions" that they've never asked for and don't value.

Here's the traditional pathway for managing survey results: Employees report they want more recognition, so an employee committee designs a multistep solution including introducing "Employee of the Month," "Employee of the Year," and "Employee Appreciation Week" initiatives, and, to recognize service, giving employees a company-logoed backpack at five years and a clock at ten.

The company then resurveys a year later and gets the same results. Why does this universally applied method fail? Because when employees complain about lack of recognition, the last thing they want to do is watch someone else receive an award. And the first thing they want is for their manager to tell them they did a good job. Your employees don't want town hall meetings or CEO videos to improve communications, or career ladders to improve development. Your employees want their direct-report manager to build trust by telling them when they do a good job, to keep them in the information loop, and to help them to grow their skills.

Employee surveys are causing HR departments all over to play whack-a-mole with each list of employee wants, developing one-size-fits-all programs that have little impact on employee engagement and employee retention. This results in the levels of inertia implied by Figure 9.

It is Gallup, by the way, that tells us that "70 percent of the variance in team engagement is determined solely by the manager."[6] And unlike exit surveys, engagement surveys require an investment of both time and money. Both can be invested better.

Why Don't Companies Focus on First-Line Supervisors to Improve Engagement?

Because they all follow other companies' "best practices" and, frankly, they don't know how to. Their best move is to ask managers to submit engagement improvement plans, only to never follow up to see if the manager executed their plans. Nor do executive teams have a critical eye to provide feedback to the manager on whether the plan would work—whether it would actually improve engagement. And worse, no one compares managers' scores from year to year in order to coach or fire those managers who don't have the required skills, energy, or interest.

If employee engagement really mattered to executive teams, they would fire a few managers each year who failed to increase their scores over time. These are the same executives who throw around terms like "culture," "best place to work," and "employer of choice," yet they saddle some of their best workers with an ill-equipped supervisor.

The Fix That Works for Engagement

Here is a pathway to develop employee engagement that works:

1. Structure your survey reporting so you get reports with scores as far down the organization chart as possible.
2. After the first administration, provide each of your first-line supervisors with a specific and measurable goal for the next survey administration.
3. Train your leaders to conduct Stay Interviews and ask them to build one-on-one engagement plans with each member of their teams.
4. Hold them accountable to achieving their goal score.
5. If they miss, ask for details about their Stay Interviews and then coach them—or replace them with a leader who can build trust with their team.

One Last Gobble: Employees Are Not Equal

Every savvy manager can immediately draw up a list of three employees he could not afford to lose, and another list of three whom he could. The gap in performance might be surprising, though, because academics have proven that your top performers produce four times more output than your average workers. Just one of many academic studies across several industries found that the top 5 percent of the workforce produced 26 percent of the participating companies' total output.[7] This means that your top performers are producing the required work for their own jobs *plus the jobs of four other employees.* You are paying them one salary to do the work of five people.

Smart companies identify their top performers and have them listed as first to receive more pay and additional training. Most importantly, they ensure they have a great boss to coach and retain them. Yet, for most companies, those who perform the most work are herded along by the same policies as others.

Individual employee engagement survey results are confidential, of course, meaning companies are basing solutions on average employee opinions and never learning what their top performers think. These top performers are also the employees who lead others by their hard-work example, are the ones others look up to, the ones others want to be like, and the ones who become the designated or undesignated leaders of your teams.

This is one more reason why companies that insist on continuing with employee surveys should have their managers conduct Stay Interviews with each employee, because these eyeball-to-eyeball conversations will disclose clearly what your top performers need to remain engaged and onboard. These individual insights will never appear in employee survey reports.

Turkey #3: External Turnover and Engagement Benchmarks

This one deserves five plump turkeys that tip the scale.

Many companies buy employee retention and employee engagement data, either as part of their engagement survey results or as a separate purchase. Those companies are already accustomed to securing benchmark data for operational areas like sales data, quality data, and more. It therefore seems right to make the same commitment to data for retention and engagement.

Let's focus first on employee engagement, where most survey companies will include comparative data in their contracts. So we begin with our data being restricted to only those companies that use the same vendor that we use. And, of course, we are also bound by that vendor's metric scale, which might be different than other vendors' scales.

To highlight this issue of measurement metrics, Gallup frequently points out that other survey vendors' scales produce higher engagement scores because Gallup grades more conservatively. For example, as we saw above, Gallup places each survey outcome into one of just three metric categories—engaged, not engaged, and actively disengaged. One of these categories is positive, the other two negative. Other vendors might place survey outcomes for example into five categories, for which two or even three might be classified as positive. Your comparative benchmark data, then, is restricted by the vendor you use.

The bigger problem, though, is that somewhere along the way *the average scores have become the goal.* Regardless of whether your employee engagement benchmark group is large or small, if the benchmark score is, let's say, 62 and your company also scores 62, then the assumption can easily become, "If others scored 62 and we scored 62, then we must be doing pretty good because our benchmark peers can't do any better, and so 62 must be the best that we can do." Or, if you beat the benchmark by one point, then you might see yourself as head of your class.

When it comes to engagement surveys then, ask your vendor to compare you to their top 10 percent, and strive to earn your way into that group.

Imagine the following contrasting conversations regarding turnover data.

Turnover-Reporting Scenario #1

> HR: Our annualized turnover is now just 18 percent, and according to benchmark data we are ahead of our peers.
> CEO: Great work, Monica!

Turnover-Reporting Scenario #2

> HR: Our annualized turnover is now just 18 percent, and according to benchmark data we are ahead of our peers.
> CEO: Great work, Monica!
> HR: This means our annualized turnover's overall costs are now down to just $6.2 million.

CEO: What did you say? Let me see those numbers. We have to do better!

Reporting turnover in percentages only is speaking a foreign language to executives whose minds are trained to think in dollars, which results in their placing more value on comparative benchmark data than they should. Reporting turnover in dollars makes fixing turnover more obvious, more of an emergency.

Many executives see turnover like rush-hour traffic, something that is inevitable so they must work around it—until they grasp turnover's cost, which drives them toward real solutions. Besides, uninformed CEOs believe turnover is driven by pay and benefits, so they feel very OK about staying in the middle of the pack rather than increasing costs. Except that pay has little to do with why employees leave, and benefits mean even less.

One Wise-Owl Idea: Reducing Managers' Spans of Control

Research supports our natural inclination that as each manager's span of control goes up, employee turnover then follows. One study reports specifically that each additional 10 employees who report to one manager will increase annual turnover by 1.6 percent.[8] And I recall reading a study way back when working with Professor Kevin Murphy (see Chapter 3) about a direct correlation between increases in nurse managers' spans of control and increased nurse turnover.

While there is no recommended number of direct reports per industry or job, it makes sense that managers on all levels including, of course, first-line supervisors, can become stretched by too many direct reports. Especially if those direct reports have high turnover, which requires that supervisor to continually hire, train, coach, and fix early errors.

I've seen evidence of this in manufacturing, call centers, and other industries, but when observing too many direct reports, no industry competes with healthcare. For whatever historical reason, the notion of aligning fifty or more nurses with one manager is repeated in aging hospitals as well as in shiny new buildings.

The daily complexities of these two jobs—nurse manager and nurse—should alone call for lower spans of control. But managing nurses is perhaps the most challenging first-line supervisor role of all, because of these reasons:

- Nurses require knowledge support because practices, policies, and equipment, along with treatments, drugs, and regulations, are continually in a swirl of change. And the "fresh outs"—the nurses who recently graduated from nursing school—need much additional training beginning on day one.
- Nurses and their managers often work different schedules because nursing is a 24/7 profession. And nurse scheduling is continually being accommodated to individual nurses' needs due to the national nursing shortage.
- Nurses choose their profession to help sick people, so at times they will have heightened emotional needs because some patients get sicker and die. Families sometimes take out emotional needs on nurses as well.
- High nurse turnover adds to the churn of hire/train/ coach/fix errors combined with the pressure to place nurses on the floor as soon as possible where hospitals need them.

Containing costs also comes into play. Overall, the high nursing spans of control are a reflection of the complex, high-stakes, and high-cost nature of healthcare delivery, with patient health and satisfaction as the critical bottom-line indicators. A 2023 study found that an estimated hundred thousand US nurses abandoned the profession during the COVID-19 pandemic, with frequent reports telling us how many will follow.[9]

Nurse manager–nurse relationships can become robotic based on all of the above. When visiting patient friends in hospitals, I usually quiz the attending nurse on her job and always ask how often that nurse sees his manager, with the most common answer being "Whenever I screw up." The problem is recurring and clear.

Each of you can imagine the challenge of asking overworked nurse managers to somehow carve out time to conduct Stay Interviews with every member of their teams. Our method is to ask during training if each manager can add as few as two Stay Interviews per week, beginning with new hires and top performers. Or even just one. If scheduling each nurse for a Stay Interview requires a full six months to do so, we have still provided a very helpful service, even if the rollout is slow.

You will read in Part Two about our work with Covenant Health in New England, an eighteen-facility healthcare company. We piloted a project there to reduce nurse manager/nurse ratios, for which we:

1. Engaged the CEO as *the* turnover champion and sponsor, who single-handedly drove accountability for both the full retention process as well as the results, including this span of control project.
2. Established a goal that each nurse supervisor would directly manage no more than thirty nurses.
3. Revisited their cost for losing one nurse, which was a very conservative $22,195.
4. Identified all of the jobs that assisted the nurse managers, including titles such as Assistant Nurse Manager, Charge Nurse, and others; these were administrative roles that at the time did not directly supervise any nurses.
5. Determined the salary grade that would be appropriate if some of these administrative jobs became first-line nurse supervisor jobs that directly managed nurses and reported up to the current overburdened nurse managers.
6. Based on the resulting salary grades, determined the amount of money to be budgeted to convert a sufficient number of these administrative jobs to supervisory jobs.
7. Gained approval for those budget additions based on the savings from forecasted lower nurse turnover.

8. Identified the specific job competencies required for the newly created position of nurse supervisor.

9. Notified the current assistant nurse managers and charge nurses that we were restructuring our nursing organization and invited them to apply for the new nursing supervisor jobs.

The resulting interviews were stringently based on the new job's competencies, with a strong lean toward coaching new and continuing nurses. Having been in a nursing administrative role was not an immediate path to the new supervisor role without having those requisite skills.

The outcome was that over time Covenant Health exceeded its targeted ratio to where each nurse supervisor directly managed no more than twenty-five nurses, and you will read later about this project's contribution to significantly reducing their nurse turnover. And, once again, the key data piece to move minds was the calculated cost of losing one nurse.

Four Key Takeaways from These Turkey and Owl Ideas

1. Exit surveys absorb much time for little actual return, and the chances of improving that process enough to make continuing to do them fruitful are slim.

2. Engagement surveys have many flaws, with the greatest of all being managers are not held accountable for improving their scores.

3. External benchmark data for turnover and engagement are sufficiently flawed that it's better to focus on improving your own data instead.

4. Where necessary, reducing manager/employee spans of control is a critical step to improving both engagement and retention.

10 ■ Why More Pay Will Never Be Enough

Let's start with this simple but meaningful scenario that requires just a little bit of imagination. After you and I have completed a series of interviews together, I am now offering you a job with these conditions:

- The duties are identical to the duties of your current job.
- You will work with the same colleagues and the same clients or patients.
- You will work in the same location whether you travel to work or you work from home.
- You will work the same schedule.
- You will have identical benefits.
- My company is on the same revenue and success trajectory as your current employer.
- And I will pay you $1 more each year.

Why would anyone leave their current job for an identical job with a pay increase that could be measured in pennies? Because in our fictional scenario we are holding all variables the same except two: your pay and your boss. And let's recall that your boss and the things your boss controls are what you talk about over dinner.

In our scenario you have spent a short time during interviews with me, and you will compare those experiences to your daily experiences with your current boss and how that flows down to working with your potential new team.

Let's now change the pay part and say I offered you a 5 percent increase over your current pay—or maybe a 5 percent decrease. How you respond depends on how much you want to leave your current boss and your current job. This is one of those examples where your exit survey leave reason would be "better opportunity" (see Chapter 9), which conveniently sidesteps any controversy that accompanies a meaningful answer.

The point of this scenario is that people don't leave jobs they like for small amounts of money. And they likely never look for another job, either. The greatest variable regarding how much most employees like their jobs is how much they like and trust their boss.

Translating this concept to this finding by Gallup, engaged employees would require a 31 percent pay increase to change jobs, whereas those who are actively disengaged require far less.[1]

A Major Data-Dig regarding Pay

The Great Resignation period was so named because such a high number of employees quit their jobs during that time, so America responded by raising pay[2] significantly during those times. Home Depot was an out-front leader, posting a letter to employees that they were investing more than $1 billion in employee pay, even as sales were slowing down.

During this time, MIT released its study on the real reasons employees were quitting their jobs. One MIT professor doubles as CEO of Revelio Labs, which studied literally millions of online employee profiles to identify employees' real quit reasons. *They concluded that pay was the sixteenth-ranked reason why employees were quitting their jobs.* The top reason, they declared, was "toxic corporate culture," which was more than ten times more powerful than compensation in predicting a company's attrition rate.[3]

MIT defined toxic corporate culture with three descriptors: (1) failure to promote diversity, equity, and inclusion; (2) workers feeling disrespected; and (3) unethical behavior. This links back to Chapter 3, where I described Gallup's reporting that the number one reason employees quit during this period was "employee engagement and culture" (41 percent) and they too cited three specific inclusions under that heading, which are (1) advancement and development opportunities, (2) not being treated with respect, and (3) unrealistic job expectations and responsibilities. Gallup said just fourteen percent of quitting employees did so because of pay.[4]

Two very respected research institutions not only placed pay way down the line as employee quit reasons, but their specific definitions of their top quit reasons squarely point their fingers at first-line supervisors as they cite disrespect, failure to advance and develop, and unrealistic job expectations.

Less credible studies note pay as at or near the top, but such studies typically survey employees or HR representatives who are likely repeating their misleading exit survey results.

Here, then, are two questions I would ask the executives of Home Depot and the thousands of other companies that raised their pay significantly during these times:

1. *Did you budget major pay increases for current employees or only for new hires?* On one hand, money matters more to those not working because they know relatively little about their prospective employer versus someone who already works there, so the amount of money offered is one known, concrete variable. Yet raising new-hire pay without raising pay for current employees would generate pay compression. This, in turn, could cause current employees to seek other jobs due to feeling such a lack of respect—even though those leaving employees might

cite "pay" or "better opportunity" as their reasons for leaving.

2. *Have your executive teams devoted as many resources to solving "toxic cultures" as you have to increasing pay?* Toxic cultures can potentially exist at the top, middle, and lower levels of an organization.

Money or Recognition?

The data above spotlight the crossover between the exit reasons of "pay," "lack of recognition," and "disrespect."

Let's use the example of an employee who gets paid $50,000 per year. Giving that employee a 5 percent out-of-cycle increase provides a real-dollar bump of about $82 per paycheck. This is hardly enough additional money to buy a new house, new vehicle, or make a major lifestyle improvement, *yet being told why you deserve such a raise and then telling your family and friends about your raise might have greater personal value.*

Flipping our example, let's suppose that an adequately performing employee learns that a peer received a raise but she did not, leading to an emotional loss and maybe less engagement and retention. And the same can be said for learning that new hires into your same job are making more money than you from day one.

More data point to employees quitting their jobs for reasons other than pay, and recent research also points to the specific pay cuts employees would gladly accept to work from home.[5]

A Job, Career, or Calling?

Yale professor Amy Wrzesniewski has studied how individuals identify with their work. Wrzesniewski has established three different work orientations, which are job, career, and calling. There is great value in studying the role of pay in each of these:

- *Job*: A job provides you with pay, benefits, and perhaps some social perks. This orientation is primarily about earning that paycheck. People in this category are typically more invested in their lives outside of work as work is merely the way they afford to do the things they love. They focus on their family, friends, and hobbies more than their professional pursuits. If you no longer see your job as a place to learn, gain experience, or increase your connections, it could be a sign that you have a "Job" orientation toward your work.

- *Career*: A job is something you do for others, while a career is what you do for yourself. Career professionals are also working for the paycheck, but they are more driven to seek out opportunities for advancement in the workplace. These individuals tend to strive for the next promotion, look for more training, and generally aim to impress. People with a "Career" orientation tend to have a long-term vision for their professional futures, set goals, and enjoy healthy competition with colleagues.

- *Calling*: Those who experience their work as a calling are most likely to feel a deep alignment between their vocation and who they are as a person. They feel a personal and emotional connection to their work. They are enthusiastic, have a sense of purpose, and are willing to work harder and longer to make a contribution. Unsurprisingly, people with a "Calling" orientation are often the most satisfied with their professional situation.[6]

You probably know people whose relationship to their job fits into each of these categories. Wrzesniewski makes clear that each of these three approaches is honorable, and that dissonance happens when we find ourselves in a category that goes against our grain. If our work falls into the "Job" category and we are pleased to finish a hard day's work and go home, we are more likely to be happy. But if we find ourselves in that same work situation but are driven to want an emotional connection to our work, as described in the "Calling" category, we are likely to be unhappy.

Compensation is of course an important component for all three of Wrzesniewski's work orientations, but it appears to be more important for some than others. Those in the "Career" category, for example, are clearly working for their current and increasingly higher paychecks, whereas those who see their work as a calling are most driven by their feeling a personal connection to their work.

Social service agencies come first to mind as organizations that should seek candidates who see their work as a calling, whereas investment bankers might want to hire career-driven employees who enjoy competing with others for more pay and other rewards. Which of the three job orientations works best for improving retention for your highest-turnover jobs?

The Impact on Minimum-Wage Workers

Most people classify American workers into two categories: exempt or nonexempt. Some might prefer white collar or blue collar. But minimum-wage workers are in their own category because many minimum-wage jobs offer little advancement opportunity.

Looking back on Wrzesniewski's work orientations, it is easy to assign minimum-wage workers the "Job" category, going to work for the money alone. Many of us would ask ourselves why else they would toil at the types of work they do, in part because we cannot imagine doing those jobs ourselves.

Mike Rose would differ. Rose is a professor at the University of California, Los Angeles, and his book *The Mind at Work* focuses on the intelligence of the American worker. Rose's "workers," though, include waitresses, hair stylists, plumbers, carpenters, and welders. His fundamental belief is that judgments of people's intelligence tend to be based on the type of work they do, giving some people an unfair rap, especially if they work in manual jobs.

Rose interviewed many incumbents for each job he studied, and here is just one example of his reporting on the mental approach that hair stylist Sharon takes with her clients after asking them to describe the cut they want:

You've got to add up all these pieces of the puzzle, and then at the end you've got to come up with a thought, OK, it's gotta be this length, it's gotta be layered here, it's got to be textured there, it can have a fringe, it can't have a fringe, you know, so the thought process goes. . . . It's not like we just start cutting. By the time I take my client to the shampoo bowl, after the consultation, I already have a little road map as to how I'm going to cut this haircut.[7]

I'm betting Sharon sees her hair-styling job as a calling.

Wrzesniewski backs up this potential for minimum-wage workers seeing their jobs as callings with two stories she learned by way of interviewing workers in hospitals. In one example, custodian Luke cleaned the room of a comatose patient a second time, entirely so that patient's father could witness the room being cleaned. The father had sat with his son for a full six months and had missed the first cleaning while on a cigarette break, so Luke saw his role as pleasing the father by cleaning the room a second time.

Another custodian named Carlotta also worked with comatose patients. Carlotta went outside of her job description by changing pictures on each patient's walls so when they "woke up" they would see something different. Carlotta was clear about the best part of her custodian job:

I enjoy entertaining patients. That's what I enjoy the most. And that is not really part of my job description. But I like putting on a show for them, per se. Dancing if there is a certain song on, I get to dance and if a talk show is on, I get to talk about that talk show or whatever. That's what I enjoy most. I enjoy making people laugh.[8]

So yes, minimum-wage workers can indeed see their jobs as their calling. And the data presented in this chapter make clear that pay alone will never be enough to engage and retain our best workers in their jobs.

Key Points on Why More Pay Will Never Be Enough
1. Employees who like their jobs require major salary increases to leave them.

2. Companies that build retention solutions on pay alone are not only wasting vast sums of money but are also disregarding the major reasons employees leave.
3. The job/career/calling model invites us to align new hires' interests with the best fit for our jobs.
4. Many minimum-wage workers bring great smarts to their jobs and can indeed see their jobs as a calling.

PART TWO

CLIENT CASE STUDIES

This section takes us from solutions to outcomes, delivering six client case studies, each selected to represent a different industry. While readers who work in these industries will immediately recognize the same retention struggles by way of the included job titles or specific retention objectives, all readers will see that the recommended solutions from Chapter 4 can be readily applied to all industries, as well to all jobs within those industries.

The client case studies are presented below, as reported by members of their executive teams:

1. Healthcare—Covenant Health: reduced turnover by 58 percent
2. Manufacturing—Clayton Homes: reduced turnover by 36 percent
3. Food processing—Wayne-Sanderson Farms: reduced turnover by 51 percent

4. Retail—Benny's Car Wash: reduced turnover by 43 percent
5. Social services—Youth Villages: reduced turnover by 46 percent
6. Federal Contractors—A highly classified retention case study

COVENANT HEALTH

Case Study 1 ■ Healthcare:
Covenant Health

Headquarters: Andover, Massachusetts, near Boston

Retention Champion: Steve Grubbs, CEO

Industry and Mission: Covenant Health is a family of eighteen
   innovative Catholic healthcare organizations with an endur-
   ing legacy of compassionate, high-quality care and deep
   roots in the communities they serve. Together their hospitals,
   skilled nursing and rehabilitation centers, assisted living
   residences, and community-based health and elder care
   organizations form a regional healthcare delivery network
   covering New England and part of Pennsylvania.

Number of employees: 5,500

Website: covenanthealth.net

Our employee retention work began in March 2021, as the organization
was emerging from financial losses and increased turnover due to
the COVID-19 pandemic, with further erosion of both predicted for

the future. Our charge was to reduce turnover and related costs across all jobs and all facilities throughout the organization. The actual cost of turnover was unclear, exit interview information was not helpful, and the then-applied employee engagement survey offered only general hints for retention actions. That survey was ultimately removed after Stay Interview implementation, which saved $200,000 annually.

The highest-turnover positions were registered nurses (RNs), licensed practical nurses, and certified nursing assistants (CNAs). Each opening required immediate replacement by using agency staffing, which cost a much higher rate. Turnover costs per exit were measured for RNs at $22,195 and for CNAs at $16,493, both of which are very conservative compared to industry comparisons.

Company-wide retention results since implementation:

- Turnover has reduced from 43 percent to 18 percent, a 58 percent improvement.
- Total dollar savings based on conservative projections equal $21.1 million.

Paige Hagerstrom serves as vice president and chief employee experience officer. Having managed this implementation closely from day one, Paige saw that while most large healthcare systems were losing even more employees due to pandemic discouragement and exhaustion, Covenant Health's turnover was decreasing instead. She also reported that a full 85 percent of managers continue to regularly complete their Stay Interviews on time, and that not one manager has been demoted nor terminated due to failure to achieve retention goals.

On Paige's best retention example:

We had a medical assistant whose manager had learned during a Stay Interview that this employee would soon quit to return to school. The manager consequently forecasted her as yellow, that she would leave within six to twelve months. But that same manager soon after participated in our Retention Accountability session where managers disclose to each other their reasons for forecasting employees to leave within the next twelve months. During that meeting another manager agreed to offer a part-time position to that employee such that she could return to school, and as a result Covenant Health would retain her as an employee. Without such focused retention attention, this employee would have become another exit who would have had to have been replaced.

With more than thirty years' experience in HR, **Tim Juergensen** was the executive who initially invited us to reduce Covenant Health's turnover.

On why Tim attacked turnover in a nontraditional way:

With the impact of COVID, our nurse turnover rose to over 32 percent and our spend on expensive travel nurses was close to $100 million. At the same time, our recruitment function was hiring more nurses and for other jobs than ever before. We knew we could not hire or buy our way out the staffing crisis that all other healthcare organizations were experiencing across the US. So our strategy had to be focused entirely on retention.

On the connection between first-line leaders and employee retention:

I learned early in my career that the research is right—that the relationship between a leader and their team members is the number-one driving factor to an employee experience that results in minimal turnover and related turnover costs, as well as organizational performance excellence. So we put our dilemma in the hands of our leaders. It was time to make what we all agreed was common sense become common practice for our leaders. Leaders who were making their goals were recognized and rewarded. Leaders who struggled were coached and developed in positive ways. Bottom-line, leader–team member relationships became a key part of a leader's day job and was *the* critical success factor in meeting and sustaining our turnover and agency cost reduction goals.

On the CEO's initial request:

Our CEO asked over one thousand leaders across our organization to sit down individually with each of their existing employees at least once a year to listen to what they enjoyed most about their work; what they were learning or wanted to learn; why they stayed; what caused them to consider leaving; and how, as a boss, we could do better. We asked leaders to have this conversation with new employees within ninety days of their start date and again at the six-month mark of employment. The key deliverable of each of these conversations was a "stay plan," that the leader and team member would work together in implementing.

On the first signs of success:

Within the first two weeks I had over one hundred emails from leaders and employees, describing the intrinsic emotional impact these conversations had on these folks, and thanking Covenant Health for investing in such an initiative. It was an immediate cultural transformation unlike I had ever seen before.

Ron Doty is president of St. Mary Health Care Center in Worcester, Massachusetts, one of the main Covenant Health facilities.

On Ron's initial reaction to conducting Stay Interviews with his team:

I remember when Stay Interviews were first introduced in a presidents' meeting. Questions were asked like "Can't we just include this in their annual reviews?" and "Why do both?" But once we started, the light went on and we all realized this is an opportunity to let our employees learn how much we care.

On whether Stay Interviews helped Ron become a better manager:

Stay Interviews helped me become a better listener. Employees work harder for someone they trust, which must be earned over time, and likeability is how you make them feel. Stay Interviews have helped all of us become better at building both.

On Stay Interviews' impact on performance:

All of us presidents have our eyes on "agency dollars spent." In the past year my long-term care facility has spent $51,612 less, all because we've solved how to reduce turnover.

On one unexpected benefit:

We are asked after each Stay Interview to identify the top reasons that employee stays and might leave. I look at this data for all employees in my hospital when considering some changes in policies and procedures, to analyze the risk versus benefits before making some important decisions.

BONUS: HOW WE LEARNED THAT STAY INTERVIEWS REDUCE WORKERS' COMPENSATION CLAIMS

Chris Clark is a senior health and safety consultant with Cove Risk Services, which provides workers' compensation insurance across the New England area. Chris called me out of the blue a few months ago to ask, "What's this Stay Interview thing?"

During a meeting with an HR executive for one of the Covenant facilities, Chris asked what contributed most to the steep decline in injury claims, and the resounding answer was "Stay Interviews." By feeling closer to their leaders, employees were not only more careful on the job but more committed to their facilities' policies and injury prevention efforts, which resulted in decreased workers' compensation claims. After connecting with the directors of two other Covenant facilities, Chris heard again there was a direct correlation between Stay Interviews and improved employee safety.

We've since partnered with Chris and his team to train their client companies' leaders on the right way to conduct Stay Interviews, all targeted toward improving retention and engagement—and now also reducing workers' compensation claims.

Case Study 2 ■ Manufacturing
Clayton Homes

Headquarters: Maryville, Tennessee, south of Knoxville

Retention Champion: Ralph Elks, Senior Director of Learning and
   Development

Industry and Mission: A Berkshire-Hathaway company, Clayton is
   a leading single-family home builder. Across the country,
   their twenty-thousand-plus team members build, sell,
   finance, and insure modern manufactured homes, modular
   homes, CrossMod® homes, site-built homes, and park model
   recreation vehicles.

Website: claytonhomes.com

Clayton Homes reached out to us after executives there had read my
book *The Power of Stay Interviews* (2012, rev. 2018). We trained their
trainers on our solution in December 2021, who then implemented
that solution across the entire home building division in April 2022, a

total of 10,200 employees at sixty locations. Clayton was attacking turnover precisely at the beginning of the period known as the Great Resignation.

Since inception, Clayton's turnover has been reduced by 36 percent. Clayton estimates the cost of losing a direct labor production team member to be $5,000, and they've measured their first-year savings alone to be $7.67 million, with continuing savings after.

Niki Schrock is Clayton's vice president of team member experience, and she shared these thoughts on their previous retention efforts:

Thinking back to 2016 and the intervening years, we focused on pay, engagement, conducting engagement surveys, and leadership development. Until then we had avoided scripting our leaders, but Stay Interviews looked like a really good idea.

Regarding how Niki gained top management's support and investment:

We met with our president and VPs and told them we needed their help, to step up their involvement, and put more resources into retention in a new way. And the president said, "Let's do it." So that was the genesis of the entire program. It had to be driven by operations at the top versus by HR.

On leveraging Stay Interview results for innovation and continuous improvement:

Our SVP for operational excellence became very interested in what ideas employees were telling their supervisors since we'd never had such a one-on-one expansive communication opportunity like this before. So we've found a way to capture these ideas and we've made our company better by doing so.

Niki's best suggestion for gaining managers' buy-in:

Don't skimp on the time required for plant managers to calculate their own cost of turnover. We taught them to use the turnover calculator rather than be told by HR how much their turnover costs them. It was so impactful because they more readily did what we asked them to do and buckled down to cut their own turnover.

Ralph Elks, Clayton's Retention Champion, made the following observations, beginning with "practicing the process":

The simplicity of the program—"ask these five questions"—still requires managers to practice many skills to do them well. The managers who practiced listening, asking follow-up questions, and writing down notes were able to experience positive impact.

On developing one-on-one stay plans for each employee:

We have completed well over 23,000 stay interviews that have resulted in 9,300 documented stay plans. We have heard of many stories of team members needing simple things like tools and resources to do their job better. We have had many stories of managers and team members learning about things that they have in common that they never knew. We have also heard stories of managers learning about specific relationship challenges that team members were having, and they were able to support and sometimes help resolve them.

Shawn Jorgensen serves as senior director of HR and has been a key stakeholder in this project. Shawn shared the following:

To report just a few of our measurable successes, thirty-five of our forty facilities reduced the number of terminations by location at the end of our first year. One of the largest drops took a facility from 199 terminations per year and lowered them to fifty-five. That obviously has a huge impact on productivity.

Regarding culture, engagement, and trust:

One of the ways I measure impact outside of the measurable data is through stories from our leaders. Throughout the years since the launch of the program, I hear how stay interviews have become a part of our culture. Leaders, frontline leaders to our most senior leaders, will share how Stay Interviews are considered a valuable tool for building trust and engagement.

On the relationship between pay and retention:

I used to never believe those studies that said pay was the fifth reason employees quit. Now I do, and supervisors failing to build trusting relationships is clearly the top turnover reason.

Case Study 3 ■ Food Processing
Wayne-Sanderson Farms

Headquarters: Oakwood, Georgia, near Atlanta

Retention Champions: One in each of the company's twenty-two complexes

Industry and Mission: Formed from two leading poultry companies with humble roots in farm supply and feed manufacturing, Wayne-Sanderson Farms is built on over a century's worth of industry expertise and excellence in operation. As the nation's third-largest poultry producer, the company has more than twenty-six thousand employees and over two thousand family farmers dedicated to delivering high-quality, affordable poultry products to customers and consumers around the world.

Website: waynesandersonfarms.com

Our work with Wayne-Sanderson began at a pilot site at the Dothan, Alabama, complex in January 2021, when COVID-19 was still highly contagious. Starting at that time was indicative of Wayne-Sanderson's recognition of how much employee turnover was hurting their business. We have since expanded our work to their total of twenty-two complexes.

Wayne-Sanderson Farms estimates the cost of losing one line associate who works on the production floor to be $8,500, and that a 1 percent company-wide turnover reduction represents a savings of $2.2 million.

- For Dothan, turnover has been reduced by 51 percent, saving $6.8 million since inception.
- Company-wide, replacement hiring was reduced by over 8,600 jobs compared to the previous year as twenty of twenty-two complexes continued to improve retention. This translates to savings of $81 million since the project's beginning.

Brad Williams is a senior director of fresh operations and directly manages five Wayne-Sanderson complexes. Brad checks weekly reports on his managers to ensure they are completing their Stay Interviews on time and that they are achieving their thirty-/sixty-/ninety-day new-hire retention goals.

Regarding the Dothan pilot's initial turnover trends:

I've been working on turnover for probably thirty years. So in the recent past, our turnover continued to increase even though the things we were doing were pretty much the same things we've been doing for a long time and been pretty successful at it. We chose the pilot location to be Dothan because historically they had very low turnover, but it had increased dramatically over the last couple of years, and to the point where it was one of the worst in the company.

On his managers' initial response to conducting Stay Interviews:

It's easy for us to say, "Do this," and in the beginning they did it because we told them to do it. The Stay Interview process takes their time away from the floor and it required some time for them to see the benefit of it, and for them to be really good at it. But once they start to do it over and over again, you see that it does work, that that effort to build relationships and build trust early on pays off in that people come to you with their issues, they communicate with you in a more honest way. So it really does build on itself.

On seeing retention as a long-term process:

This is not a silver bullet as it's more like a silver plough. But this plough won't do you any good in the barn because the only time it does any good is when you're working it. And whether you are cultivating the earth with a plough or building your team, building trust is the only way you get it done. You have to do it.

David Malfitano is the now-retired top HR executive who initially reached out to our company for retention help. David's thoughts on calculating the cost of turnover:

We invited respected finance and operations leaders to participate in calculating the cost of turnover so the result wouldn't be seen as "HR's number"... and also so that Stay Interviews and accountability wouldn't be seen as an HR fix. Operations must own it.

Regarding "doing his own drywall":

At first we tried training leaders to do Stay Interviews on our own but didn't really know how. Then we brought in the experts because we didn't understand the importance of both the specific training details as well as holding leaders accountable for building individual stay plans and for making their retention goals.

On how risk-taking built company-wide commitment:

I committed to our board of directors that we would reduce turnover in our Dothan pilot location by 20 percent in one year... and few in operations outside of that location believed it was possible. Then once we exceeded that target, the other locations started giving up their excuses and instead focused on proper implementation.

And on one underused tactic to reduce new-hire turnover:

> One thing I learned was to consistently ask candidates for a "one-year commitment" during the hiring process. It starts during the initial phone-screen and must continue through onboarding and via our supervisors during each employee's first few weeks.

Kinia Curtis is a thirty-two-year employee currently serving as sanitation manager in the Union Springs, Alabama, complex. On the project's initial success, Kinia reported "amazing results" that "reduce[d] turnover from 256 percent to 78 percent in two years."

On retaining new hires:

> I set limits on how many new hires I could take on at any given time, regardless of how many openings we had, because I knew I had to conduct Stay Interviews and do hands-on training with them in order to make my new-hire retention goal.

Kinia's greatest lesson learned:

> Conducting Stay Interviews forced me to listen, so I learned that every employee really is different and has different needs on the job.

Lily Brooks is the HR manager for the Waco, Texas, complex where annualized turnover has been reduced from 174 percent to 80 percent in less than one year. Stay Interviews are conducted with new hires on their fifth and fifteenth days, and supervisors schedule Stay Interviews with three continuing employees each week.

Lily's thoughts on the greatest operations improvement since turnover has decreased:

> The Waco complex has been able to fully staff both shifts, resulting in the conversion of an automated rapid line with a cone line. So we've improved product quality and yield as well as reduced maintenance costs.

And on employee relationships:

It really is all about building supervisor and employee trust. Now employees are coming forward with solutions instead of problems, which is a new thing here.

Sherri Merbach of C-Suite Analytics loves to tell this story:

The Dothan leadership team searched out ways to drive supervisory accountability for retention, and their answer was to glue a sticker on the front of each supervisor's helmet that presented their retention goals in a way that only those Dothan leaders could understand. So their annual and new-hire retention goals were always literally in their faces when speaking with one another or looking in the restroom mirror.

Wayne-Sanderson's then-VP of Field Human Resources **Bill Love** concludes with the following:

The magic for me is that this solution provides a process to guide you in doing the right thing. So if you honor the process the metrics take care of themselves. Anytime we see a location not achieving turnover, you can almost bet that they are not following the process somewhere. It becomes easier for us to address because we can inspect each piece to determine where we should get back on course.

Case Study 4 ■ Retail
Benny's Car Wash

Headquarters: Baton Rouge, Louisiana

Retention Champion: Katherine Barker, Chief Human Resources
Officer

Industry and Mission: Since opening their first car wash location
in 1951, Benny's car care services have expanded to include
detailing, oil changes, and state inspections, along with
B-Quik convenience stores and fueling stations, with nine
locations serving the Baton Rouge area. The times, the
technology, and the cars have changed, but the values of this
family-owned and operated establishment remain the same.

Number of employees: 400

Website: bennyscarwash.com

We began working with Benny's in September 2022, focusing on reducing turnover among all jobs. The highest turnover was among customer service associates in the retail stores and in the car wash. The

initial goals were to reduce annual turnover by 25 percent and to improve new-hire retention by retaining 90 percent of new hires in their first sixty days.

Turnover across all jobs since inception has decreased by 43 percent, with total annual savings equal to $518,000. Benny's estimates the average cost per exit across all jobs to be $3,500.

Katherine Barker is the top HR executive who volunteered to take on the Retention Champion role. She has successfully managed this initiative as a top operations executive would. Here are her thoughts on the greatest drivers of Benny's retention success.

On Benny's Stay Interview schedule:

Our managers conduct Stay Interviews with new employees at thirty days and another Stay Interview at six months, as well as annually for all employees. Important though is that our managers also do a Stay Interview when we believe an employee has underlying issues to address, driven in part by that manager wanting to meet her employee retention goals.

On managers' initial reaction to being assigned Stay Interviews:

Let's say that "reluctant" is a good word. It was seen as having another thing to do. Our managers are young, and their reaction reflected their misunderstanding of their roles. They have grown so much over the past couple of years because doing Stay Interviews brought them closer to their teams. They've learned their roles are to facilitate the growth of their teams versus dictate tasks to them. We could not have just told them this but instead they had to have the Stay Interview experience to learn it on their own.

On the best employee "save," the best Stay Interview experience:

One of our best managers stuck to asking the Stay Interview questions just as he was trained to do, and by doing so he learned that one employee who had been mostly quiet was instead feeling isolated, both at work and at home. That manager immediately saw that he was that employee's at-work lifeline, so he talks and listens to him carefully. And that employee is now one of our best performers.

On the best overall lesson for the young management team:

The first-line management role has evolved so much here. We now understand that employee engagement has nothing to do with an annual event but is instead the ongoing collaboration and inclusivity for all employees to contribute and continue to learn, to develop. And our managers are OK with the uncomfortable conversations that are needed to solicit the real truth from their teams.

Youth VILLAGES®
The force for families

Case Study 5 ■ Social Services
Youth Villages

Headquarters: Memphis, Tennessee

Retention Champion: Cliff Reyle, Chief of Staff, with thirty-four
   years of service

Industry and Mission: Youth Villages is a national leader in
   children's mental and behavioral health. Founded in 1986, the
   organization's 3,600-plus employees help more than 43,000
   children annually across 23 states. Youth Villages has been
   recognized by the Harvard Business School and U.S. News &
   World Report, and was identified by the White House as one
   of the nation's most promising results-oriented nonprofit
   organizations.

Website: youthvillages.org

Our employee retention work with Youth Villages began in January 2023
and has grown into two separate projects:

- Bill's Place is an intensive residential treatment program for children who must be helped in a secure setting for their personal safety. There are three hundred employees working for Bill's Place, and the highest-turnover job is teacher counselors, who are college-graduate, direct-care staff who teach, encourage, motivate, inspire, heal, and nurture their young people. They are the first to dry tears and to manage anger and other emotions. By way of our turnover cost algorithm, the cost of losing one teacher counselor is $46,095.
- The West Tennessee Program provides help for children in homes, schools, and in their neighborhoods. About two hundred employees work in the West Tennessee Program, and their highest-turnover job is family intervention specialists, who provide 24/7 in-home counseling services for high-risk youth and families in their home environment using an evidence-based approach for long-term success. The cost for losing one family intervention specialist is $16,665.

Retention results for Bill's Place: Turnover has decreased by 46 percent, representing an annual dollar saving of $4,978,260.

Retention results for the West Tennessee Program: Turnover has decreased by 37 percent, representing an annual dollar saving of $449,955.

Cliff Reyle serves as the Retention Champion, and said this about getting their retention initiative started:

> For someone who has spent 35 years in human resources, every time I heard Dick Finnegan give a presentation I knew I was hearing common sense, uncommonly applied. The Stay Interview process has provided a framework based on proven principles that a manager at any level of our organization can implement and see lasting results. Within weeks we started to reap the fruit of that engagement with lower turnover and longer retention.

Nicole Fannin is executive director of the residential division, including Bill's Place, having served Youth Villages for twenty-three years. Nicole defined her retention role as "serving as an accountability partner for leaders." Doing so includes providing high-level oversight plus being "chairman of enthusiasm and the champion for excitement and buy-in."

Nicole offered the following thoughts on her team's multiple-year development to implement Finnegan's Arrow by holding managers accountable for both facilitating Stay Interviews according to a defined schedule *and* achieving their retention goals.

On Stay Interview participation and acceptance of retention accountability:

> We had approximately 70 percent of the managers who were on board and about 30 percent who struggled with the concept. Some were intimidated and made the interviews more stressful than they needed to be. The change agent for us was that we had 100 percent buy-in with 0 percent reluctance from the directors and assistant directors, and they were able to positively influence those who struggled to get on board initially. Within a couple of months we were all on the same page at the same time.

On knowing when managers had fully bought in:

> When staff saw Stay Interviews as more casual chats and check-ins with their staff, where they could explore relationship issues versus policies or training. Relationships became stronger, there was more trust, and a different level of commitment to their staff. Each person completing the interviews had ownership and wanted to see their staff happy and thriving. This was the moment we had been waiting for! We then watched our turnover numbers improve month after month.

On the best retention story that comes to mind:

> We had a staff member who felt that she was not making an impact. During a Stay Interview she identified the things that she enjoyed about her work, so we challenged her to incorporate those things in the form of a project. She focused initially on housekeeping by creating a huge banner with a warm message and posted it on the wall in the laundry room along with a dessert table with sweet treats and snack baskets for the housekeeping staff to enjoy.

On how Nicole's own Stay Interviews with her direct reports changed her:

These relaxed questions made it easy to give my team the much-needed space to explore their "why." When you can connect to your "why," the job becomes a mission and not a task. As a result, I've become very motivated to provide that space for my leaders, which has been incredibly rewarding.

On the single-greatest benefit of reducing employee turnover:

We were able to focus on higher-level objectives with more of our top-to-bottom staff by involving them in strategic planning and long-term goal setting. Frequent turnover drives our managers to focus on training, coaching, and job fundamentals to get new hires proficient in their roles. But now we have tenured leaders and tenured employees who can carry on the culture we've worked so hard to build.

Angela McCrady is a program manager for the West Tennessee Program and is a twenty-year Youth Villages employee. Angela sees that all leaders complete their Stay Interviews on time, helps her leaders address specific retention issues, and continues to complete her Stay Interviews with her direct reports.

On the biggest change Angela has seen with her supervisors:

They now understand that whatever was being done prior was not working, and that our Stay Interviews have helped each of them build a trusting relationship with each member of their teams.

On whether managers have been demoted or terminated based on their retention-against-goal performance:

No, we have not demoted or terminated any managers based on an inability to meet retention goals. There has been more focus on helping managers engage with their employees during the Stay Interview process and how to interpret the information they receive to build impactful stay plans.

On Angela's experience with Stay Interviews in the past:

I have been doing what I thought were Stay Interviews for many years, with every employee in all of my programs, including specialists and clinical supervisors. And then I would take the information back to their supervisors to suggest how they could help. What I was missing was the impact of each supervisor completing Stay Interviews with their direct reports.

On her supervisors' greatest Stay Interview win:

We've permitted them to have one-on-one valuable time with each individual employee. Our leaders are so focused on the business aspect of things that it is hard to just sit and focus on your staff. This process has allowed them to stop everything else going on around them and focus solely on the purpose of retaining their own staff.

On Stay Interview success stories that come to mind:

We've learned that our employees really do have a life outside of work. Being in helping professions means we must avoid our natural tendency to advise them and instead limit our responses to providing emotional support and maybe restructuring assignments or schedules. But we've now supported many employees regarding home issues that we wouldn't have learned about without conducting our Stay Interviews.

On the connection between Stay Interviews and Youth Villages' annual employee survey:

We all know that surveys' biggest shortcoming is employees don't feel like anything changes as a result. With Stay Interviews our employees are right in front of us, telling us what is most important to them. So we actually make things better and they participate in our doing so.

On managers improving their accuracy when forecasting how long each employee will stay:

This improves naturally over time. Stay Interviews deepen our relationships such that employees become even more open later, plus we learn to watch for behavioral cues about staying or leaving and ask about them.

Case Study 6 ■ Federal Contractors

A Highly Classified Retention Case Study

Federal Contractors provide services to our US government, and those services range from airplane mechanics to landscapers with many jobs in between. Our company has worked with many federal contractors, and that work usually remains confidential and sometimes requires earning a federal security clearance. This case study and its outcome are about our providing retention outcomes for one of those "in-between" assignments.

We were told that a specific contract included forty managers who were actually on the payroll of other companies, the companies where they sit and provide daily services. This contract had a project executive within the federal contracting company, and this person realized that the very high turnover among those employees who worked for those forty managers was a great barrier to productivity. And those forty managers were semi-managers because they had similar job assignments to those of their teams. That's all we knew.

Nonetheless, we trained those forty managers to conduct Stay Interviews and negotiated a schedule for them to do so. Some were openly reluctant given that they perceived their relationships to be more as peers, and objected to the time involved.

I learned just a bit more about the targeted jobs when during a meeting one of the top executives apparently forgot that I didn't have security clearance. Our conversation went like this:

PROJECT EXECUTIVE: We now have about 70 percent of our managers conducting Stay Interviews, and we like the results so far.
ME: So how can we get the others to do their Stay Interviews?
MANAGER IN THE ROOM: Some of them are really distracted, like the ones in Ukraine.

This meeting was two months after the Russian invasion in February 2022.

The final project results as calculated by the project executive were that any employee who had just one Stay Interview was 75 percent more likely to stay for at least one additional year.

Closing Thoughts

Company Culture Made Easy

Everything written in this book is about improving employee retention, all in the shadow of our continually decreasing number of workers relative to our projected economic growth as presented in Chapter 1. Reducing employee turnover is not just about retaining staff. The bigger picture is about transforming your organization's culture, making it a place where loyalty fuels excellence and boosts your bottom line.

Making the connection between culture and people management is every company's objective, stated or implied. But corporate culture remains a fuzzy term with no agreed-upon definition and zero spot-on metrics. Every company wants a good one, whatever a good one is. And there is a general belief that companies that create good cultures make more money.

What do we want our cultures to be? *Harvard Business Review* published a study where organizations selected from eight culture descriptions to prioritize their own cultural preferences.[1] The overwhelming choices were (1) results and goal achievement, named by 89 percent of participating companies; and (2) a caring, warm, and collaborative culture, chosen by 63 percent. The remaining culture descriptions such as "learning," "safety," and "authority" garnered no more than 15 percent of organizations' self-preference votes. So, we all agree we want to achieve company goals while playing nice. Who wouldn't want to work for such a company?

If productivity and collaboration are what we want, the questions we need to ask are:

- How do we distinguish ourselves from other organizations when hiring, engaging, and retaining the very best talent?
- How do we *really* make ourselves different?

The Culture Hole Is at the Bottom

There is a Grand Canyon–sized hole in the way corporations execute their cultures—and that hole is at the bottom. It is customary for organizations to hire McKinsey or other gold-standard consulting firms to guide their executives through the culture identification process and then to survey and focus-group employees to develop a plan to fill those culture gaps. That plan is then presented to the corporation's board of directors with upscale graphics, and all ultimately believe the implementation trail from top to bottom is totally within view.

But that execution, along with each projected profit improvement, reaches fruition only if the employees who sell and deliver your services buy in. And their buy-in is 100 percent contingent upon the quality of their direct supervisors. Here's what Gallup has to say about supervisors' impact on our carefully articulated corporate cultures:

- Companies choose the wrong managers 82 percent of the time.[2]
- And—you'll remember this one—those same managers account for 70 percent of the variance in employee engagement.[3]

Gallup goes on to share how these data drive the lack of top-to-bottom culture-building success:

A major challenge for leaders of large organizations is that there is no common culture—often even in prominent, highly regarded companies. This is true regardless of those organizations' lofty mission statements that are written to bind all employees toward a common purpose.[4]

Making things darker, Bain & Company tells us that "culture clash" is the number one reason mergers and acquisitions fail.[5] *Harvard Business Review*, meanwhile, says failure to manage and motivate employees is one reason why 70 percent to 90 percent of acquisitions fail.[6] Or, said more plainly, your culture goes nowhere if your employees—and especially your top performers—don't buy in, fully engage, and stay.

Top performers need *great* supervisors, tens on ten-point scales. As noted in Chapter 9, top performers produce four times the output of average workers. But your top performers are scattered across many supervisors, including your best and your worst. How effectively the corporate culture impacts you as an employee depends on which supervisor you get, and for many this is based on whether you figuratively draw a long straw or a short straw on your first day of work.

We would all agree there has been far too much talk about corporate culture and far too little doing. Consultants and academics have had their say about defining and forming a specific kind of culture, but common sense tells us victory lies in the implementation at the bottom of our organization charts. What does it matter if your board of directors sees a three-colored chart of your five-year corporate culture plan if Larry the team lead is managing by instinct alone?

Culture requires consistency regarding the application of processes and policies, and, more importantly, regarding the messages that supervisors say and that first-line employees hear. And even if those messages are delivered accurately, the degree to which they are put into action hinges on the single variable of *how much that employee trusts his or her supervisor.*

Our teams need more guidance, and they want more, too. Employees join the workforce at a young age, chronologically and developmentally. Few parents or teachers instruct them on how to identify the right employer; how to manage boss relationships; how to develop a learning plan for themselves; or how to handle the intricacies of pay, work relationships, and the rest. Employees are then left to manage their work lives by instinct first and by trial and error second, which requires lost years of errors to learn the right lessons—if they learn the right lessons at all.

Here, then, is one more reminder of what employees talk about over dinner: *Bosses, colleagues, and duties.* Not pet insurance, nor any event with food. And they hardly ever discuss their pay or their benefits unless someone is sick. What your employees talk about over dinner is your corporate culture's red zone. Whatever you *say* your corporate culture is, *this is what it really is.* Now is a good time to recall Peter Drucker's quote about culture eating strategy for breakfast.[7]

Today's times are unprecedented in that we are flat running out of workers, and there remain questions as to what percentage of those workers available to us will be good ones, the ones we want to keep. Company cultures represent our operating styles, that organization in the mirror that we really are. From today forward, trustworthy one-on-one supervisor–employee relationships top to bottom must form the chassis upon which your culture is placed.

Think of this book as the culture-building flatcar on board the express train that will take your business toward *a better everything.* Whether your goals are about revenue, productivity, sales, safety, or whatever, the direct pathway to achieving them must begin with keeping the people you need to keep. Some will be the four-times-as-productive top players, while others will be just truly adequate at their jobs—and it's likely these can-do employees will become harder and harder to find.

Stay Interviews build the pathway to the caring, warm, collaborative cultures that most companies want. By doing so, they increase goal achievement, which is the other most-wanted company culture piece. And their guardrail metrics of achieving retention goals and forecasting how long each employee will stay keep your leaders focused on the most important measurements for their teams. Winning companies will make clear choices about who they want to keep and then keep them.

The Required Courage to Change

This book is also about discipline. Implementing the recommendations here requires vanquishing traditional exit and engagement surveys and installing the regimental requirements of converting turnover to dollars, establishing and building accountability for retention goals, and mandating that leaders conduct Stay Interviews effectively and on schedule.

These changes require more guts than smarts because the guidebook is here. Please write if I can help at dfinnegan@c-suiteanalytics .com.

I invite you to compare your answers to the following twelve questions regarding key points in this book with mine. Critical thinking is required to answer the majority of these questions because while the book's contents address each of the included subjects, the correct answer might not be explicitly provided. Here is an example:

Which of the following employee groups have the greatest need
for Stay Interviews and for 1-to-1 coaching?
A. Those in the military
B. Black employees
C. Those in poverty
D. Gen Z and millennial employees

The correct answer here is C, those in poverty, because they are likely to be the least skilled compared to the other groups to survive and then thrive in a typical work environment. This response is based on my own judgment versus research, and it's possible you will have a different opinion.

Once you've completed the quiz you can find my responses at c-suiteanalytics.com/targetingturnoverbook.

Good luck!

1. Which component in the Finnegan's Arrow retention model has the greatest impact on cutting turnover?
    A. Accountability because leaders knowing they must achieve retention goals will bring their stronger focus to all other retention initiatives.
    B. Stay Interviews because they are *the* supervisor–employee link for which supervisors are trained to conduct precisely.
    C. Calculating turnover's cost, which makes turnover a business issue at the executive level.
    D. Forecasting because it is the one component that causes supervisors to focus on not only Stay Interviews but also on the daily signals from their employees.

2. Which Stay Interview skill is the most important for retaining employees?
    A. Listening because supervisors who can't focus will miss important information and emotions.
    B. Probing because doing so drives the conversation from general and superficial topics to more specific and important ones.
    C. Taking notes because supervisors will not only forget key points, but they also will need notes to organize their stay plans later.
    D. Taking accountability because blaming others for employees' concerns won't lead to helpful solutions.

3. Which of the following pieces of future demographic information should bring the most concern?
    A. The continued influx of immigrants requires more awareness, more planning, and more dollars to address language and cultural issues.
    B. The anticipated additional increase of entrepreneurs means that organizations will have an even more depleted talent pool for hiring new employees.

    C. Grit-level comparisons between baby boomers and younger generations bring worry that younger employees won't work as hard.

    D. The expected number of available workers compared to the necessary ongoing improvement in America's GDP is a threat to not only our leading place among the world's economies but also to each individual company.

4. Which is the greatest reason why employee engagement has stagnated for the past twenty-plus years?

    A. External factors like George Floyd's murder and our fluctuating economy impacts the way employees think and how they work.

    B. Survey results lead to one-size-fits-all company programs that have a limited impact on how much employees engage and how long they stay.

    C. Young workers value psychological safety and are stifled without it.

    D. Leaders on all levels are not held accountable for improving their engagement scores.

5. Which is a not-so-obvious reason why employee referrals stay longer?

    A. Referring employees don't want to embarrass themselves by referring an incompetent colleague.

    B. Referred candidates already know the pluses and minuses of the job based on conversations with the referring employee.

    C. Referred candidates already have a friend at work.

    D. Supervisors focus more on retaining referred employees.

6. Which societal trend over the past twenty years has had the most impact on people's distancing themselves from others as measured by mental health statistics, as well as the reluctance for romantic relationships, sex, and maybe even fewer children?

    A. Smartphones

    B. The COVID-19 pandemic

    C. Economic conditions brought on by inflation and other wealth-threatening factors

    D. An increasing number of women joining the workforce

7. Psychologists have identified several behaviors that lead each of us to live happier lives. Which of those principles is included in this book?

    A. Practice optimism.

    B. Communicate gratitude.

    C. See life events as both good and bad, intertwined.

    D. Do kind acts.

8. Which is the most applicable outcome for our knowing that top performers out-perform average performers by 4 to 1?

    A. We should replace all average performers with top performers.

    B. Companies should identify top performers and hold supervisors accountable for retaining them.

    C. Engagement surveys are less useful because they lump together data from all employees versus separate out top-performer data.

    D. Top performers should be fast-tracked for bigger roles.

9. Which is the most important action for making desired corporate cultures become real?

    A. Leaders top to bottom reinforce the desired culture with their actions and their words.

    B. Culture messages are delivered directly to employees electronically and visually throughout their workplaces.

    C. Executives and their associated board of directors agree on specific approaches that separate their company from their competitors.

    D. Leaders and employees who act consistently with the desired culture are recognized publicly, so others follow their leads.

10. Which has the greatest value for converting turnover percentages to dollars?
    A. Leaders learn the true value of retaining versus losing an employee.
    B. Finance partners with HR to develop effective retention solutions.
    C. Turnover reports contain dollars lost, which motivates HR to build better retention solutions.
    D. Executives see the cost of turnover, which motivates them to enact retention solutions through their leadership teams versus through HR.

11. Which is the best way to measure whether a job candidate sees their work as a job, a career, or a calling?
    A. Ask what achievements made them feel best in their past three jobs.
    B. Note how often they changed jobs versus being loyal to one or a few employers.
    C. Listen for how often they voluntarily reference pay or promotions.
    D. Ask what parts of their job are most attractive to them.

12. Which is the most important outcome for Stay Interview Q3, "Why do you stay here?"
    A. This question elicits a positive response before the supervisor asks Q4 about the last time they considered leaving.
    B. By combining this response with their response to Q1, the supervisor now knows what aspects of the job make the employee most happy.
    C. The supervisor can seek out opportunities to make positive job experiences happen more frequently for the employee.
    D. Responding to this question requires the employee to discover why they stay and then hear themselves say it.

Notes

Chapter 1

1. Data sourced from the US Bureau of Labor Statistics (https://www.bls.gov/), for the periods noted.

2. Marc LaBonte, *The Federal Reserve's Response to COVID-19: Policy Issues*, Congressional Research Service Report No. R46411, February 8, 2021, https://crsreports .congress.gov/product/pdf/R/R46411/7.

3. Sources for US population data and projections (ages 18–64): Years 2000–2009: US Census Bureau, "Table 1. Intercensal Estimates of the Resident Population by Sex and Age for the United States, Regions, States, and Puerto Rico: April 1, 2000, to July 1, 2010," September 2011, https://www.census.gov/data/tables/time-series/demo/popest /intercensal-2000-2010-state.html; Years 2010–2019: US Census Bureau, "Annual Estimates of the Resident Population for Selected Age Groups by Sex for the United States, States, and Puerto Rico: July 1, 2019," December 2019, https://www.census.gov/data /tables/time-series/demo/popest/2010s-national-detail.html; Year 2020: US Census Bureau, "Annual Estimates of the Resident Population for Selected Age Groups by Sex for the United States, April 1, 2020, to July 1, 2022," June 2023, https://www.census.gov /data/tables/time-series/demo/popest/2020s-national-detail.html; Years 2025–2045: US Census Bureau, "Table 2: Projected Population by Age Group and Sex for the United States," November 2023, https://www.census.gov/data/tables/2023/demo/popproj/2023 -summary-tables.html. All sources were recommended to me by US Census Bureau demographer Jonathan Vespa via an email exchange between June 30, 2023, and March 7, 2024.

4. Jonathan Vespa, Lauren Medina, and David M. Armstrong, *Demographic Turning Points for the United States: Population Projections for 2020 to 2060*, US Census Bureau Report No. P25-1144, February 2020, https://www.census.gov/library/publicat ions/2020/demo/p25-1144.html.

5. Kara Dennison, "The Silver Tsunami Is on the Way: How Companies Can Prepare," *Forbes*, October 11, 2023, https://www.forbes.com/sites/karadennison/2023/10/11/the-silver-tsunami-is-on-the-way-how-companies-can-prepare/?sh=1af of6c3774e.

6. Beth Ann Mayer, "Americans Aren't Having Kids Because It Costs Too Much, New Study Finds," Parents, February 29, 2024, https://www.parents.com/americans-arent-having-kids-because-of-cost-8601528.

7. Daniel Cox, "The Societal Cost of the Marriage Decline," Institute for Family Studies, March 5, 2024, https://ifstudies.org/blog/the-societal-cost-of-the-marriage-decline; Bella DePaulo, "Half of All Single People Just Don't Want a Relationship," *Psychology Today*, March 23, 2024, https://www.psychologytoday.com/nz/blog/living-single/202008/half-of-all-single-people-just-dont-want-a-relationship.

8. Emily Willingham, "People Are Having Less Sex Whether They Are Teenagers or 40-Somethings," January 23, 2002, *Scientific American*, https://www.scientificamerican.com/article/people-have-been-having-less-sex-whether-theyre-teenagers-or-40-somethings/.

9. US Census Bureau, "US Population to Begin Declining in Second Half of Century," press release no. CB23-189, November 9, 2023, https://www.census.gov/newsroom/press-releases/2023/population-projections.html.

10. Jerome H. Powell, "Inflation and the Labor Market," speech, Hutchins Center on Fiscal and Monetary Policy, Brookings Institution, Washington, DC, November 30, 2022, https://www.federalreserve.gov/newsevents/speech/powell20221130a.htm.

11. John Elfein, "Number of Coronavirus Disease 2019 (COVID-19) Deaths in the U.S. as of June 14, 2023, by Age," Statista, June 21, 2023, https://www.statista.com/statistics/1191568/reported-deaths-from-covid-by-age-us/.

12. "New Business Surge: Unveiling the Business Application Boom through an Analysis of Administrative Data," *White House Blog*, January 11, 2024, https://www.whitehouse.gov/cea/written-materials/2024/01/11/new-business-surge-unveiling-the-business-application-boom-through-an-analysis-of-administrative-data/.

13. Jim Harter, "US Engagement Hits 11-Year Low," Gallup, April 10, 2024, https://www.gallup.com/workplace/643286/engagement-hits-11-year-low.aspx.

14. Tim Paradis, "Gen Zers Are Saying 'No Thanks' to Promotions for Reasons That Go Beyond Money," *Business Insider*, November 8, 2023, https://www.businessinsider.com/gen-z-rejects-promotions-management-roles-traditional-corporate-ladder-2023-11; Orianna Rosa Royal, "Gen Zers Are Treating Employers Like Bad Dates," *Fortune*, February 19, 2024, https://fortune.com/europe/2024/02/19/gen-z-job-interview-ghosting-indeed/.

15. "Half of Young Workers Report Mental Health Challenges," *APA Blogs*, January 30, 2023, https://www.psychiatry.org/news-room/apa-blogs/half-of-young-workers-report-mental-health-challen.

16. Jean Sahadi, "Many Parents Say They Are Still Financially Subsidizing Their Adult Children," CNN Business, January 25, 2024, https://www.cnn.com/2024/01/25/success/parenting-adult-children-living-home/index.html.

17. Tom Swiderski and Sarah Crittenden Fuller, "Student GPA and Test Score Gaps Are Growing—and Could Be Slowing Pandemic Recovery," Brookings Institution, November 6, 2023, https://www.brookings.edu/articles/student-gpa-and-test-score-gaps-are-growing-and-could-be-slowing-pandemic-recovery/; Alec MacGillis, "Skipping School: America's Hidden Education Crisis," ProPublica, January 8, 2024, https://www.propublica.org/article/school-absenteeism-truancy-education-students; Sarah Hernholm, "Rise of Homeschooling Is Making a Transformative Impact on Education," Forbes, May 2, 2024, https://www.forbes.com/sites/sarahhernholm/2024/04/30/rise-of-homeschooling-and-its-transformative-impact-on-education/.

18. Jean M. Twenge, "Have Smart Phones Destroyed a Generation?," The Atlantic, September 2017, https://www.theatlantic.com/magazine/archive/2017/09/has-the-smartphone-destroyed-a-generation/534198/.

19. "Millennials or Gen Z: Who's Doing the Most Job-Hopping," CareerBuilder Blog, accessed March, 10, 2025, https://www.careerbuilder.com/advice/blog/how-long-should-you-stay-in-a-job.

20. "75% of Businesses Have Been Affected by the Labor Shortage," New Jersey Business Magazine, October 24, 2022, https://njbmagazine.com/njb-news-now/75-of-businesses-have-been-affected-by-the-labor-shortage/.

21. Timothy Nerozzi, "American Airlines Drops 3 Cities from Service, Blaming Pilot Shortage, 'Soft Demand,'" Fox Business, January 7, 2023, https://www.foxbusiness.com/lifestyle/american-airlines-drops-3-cities-service-blaming-pilot-shortage-soft-demand; Andrew Tangel and Alison Sider, "Your Pilot Has a New Job—and a Bigger Plane to Fly," Wall Street Journal, November 7, 2023, https://www.wsj.com/business/airlines/airlines-pilots-planes-safety-united-delta-southwest-e438ce08?st=kkg8q2fpzxjkhab.

22. Sharon Terlep and Sarah Nassauer, "CVS, Walmart to Cut Pharmacy Hours as Staffing Squeeze Continues," Wall Street Journal, January 27, 2023, https://www.wsj.com/articles/cvs-walmart-to-cut-pharmacy-hours-as-staffing-squeeze-continues-11674796388.

23. Noah Schwartz, "Labor Shortages, Supply Chain Issues Delay Opening of Arizona Hospital," Beckers Hospital Review, November 22, 2023, https://www.beckershospitalreview.com/capital/labor-shortages-supply-chain-issues-delay-opening-of-arizona-hospital.html.

24. Evie Blad, "A District's Bus 'Disaster' Highlights a Nationwide Driver Shortage," Education Week, August 15, 2023, https://www.edweek.org/leadership/a-districts-bus-disaster-highlights-a-nationwide-driver-shortage/2023/08.

25. Rose Khattar and Maureen Coffey, "The Child Care Sector Is Still Struggling to Hire Workers," Center for American Progress, October 19, 2023,

https://www.americanprogress.org/article/the-child-care-sector-is-still-struggling-to
-hire-workers/.

26. Rachel Wallen Oglesby, "Eliminating Unnecessary Degree Requirements
from Public Sector Careers," America First Policy Institute, October 25, 2024, https://
americafirstpolicy.com/issues/eliminating-unnecessary-degree-requirements-from
-public-sector-careers.

27. Stephen Elliott, "Republicans Push for Teenagers as Young as 14 to Work in
Restaurants, Industrial Jobs," *USA Today*, April 18, 2023, https://www.usatoday
.com/story/news/nation/2023/04/18/child-labor-laws-targeted-lawmakers-11-states
-seek-weaken/11682548002/; Ariana Figueroa, "States Seek to Let Teens as Young as 14
Serve Booze in Restaurants," *Oregon Capital Chronicle*, August 10, 2023, https://
oregoncapitalchronicle.com/2023/08/10/states-seek-to-let-teens-as-young-as-14-serve
-booze-in-restaurants/.

28. "Bonuses," MyArmyBenefits (US Army), last modified February 28, 2024,
https://myarmybenefits.us.army.mil/Benefit-Library/Federal-Benefits/Bonuses
?serv=122; Rachel S. Cohen, "Fatter Recruits Now Welcome as Air Force Revises
Its Rules," *Air Force Times*, April 4, 2023, https://www.airforcetimes.com/news
/your-air-force/2023/04/03/fatter-recruits-now-welcome-as-air-force-revises-its
-rules/.

29. Cohen, "Fatter Recruits Now Welcome as Air Force Revises its Rules."

30. James Tutten, "Shortage of Garbage Truck Drivers Leads to Recycling Items
Piling Up in Altamonte Springs," WFTV Channel 9, July 13, 2023, https://www.wftv
.com/news/local/shortage-garbage-truck-drivers-leads-recycling-items-piling-up
-altamonte-springs/62NSVILQFJFNBGEMDEXUZ3RWOU/.

31. Jeff Levkulich, "Seminole County Sheriff Lowers Minimum Age for Detention
Deputies in Hopes of Filling Positions," WFTV Channel 9, November 17, 2023,
https://www.wftv.com/news/local/seminole-county-sheriff-lowers-minimum-age
-detention-deputies-hopes-filling-positions/7R4V4BBY55ED5AP3LZNQY53FXQ/.

32. Serah Lewis, "'The Future of Our Economy': Workers with Criminal Rec-
ords Are a Massive Untapped Talent Pool, Business Leaders Argue. Here's Why
Giving Them a Break Can Be a Big Win for All," Moneywise, October 6, 2023,
https://moneywise.com/employment/employment/employing-the-formerly-incar
cerated.

33. Harry J. Holzer, "Understanding the Impact of Automation on Workers, Jobs,
and Wages," Brookings Institution, January, 19, 2022, https://www.brookings.edu
/blog/up-front/2022/01/19/understanding-the-impact-of-automation-on-workers
-jobs-and-wages/.

34. Vespa, Medina, and Armstrong, *Demographic Turning Points*, 1.

35. "Immigration," Gallup, accessed January 31, 2025, https://news.gallup.com
/poll/1660/immigration.aspx.

36. Alex Nowrasteh, "15 Myths about Immigration De-Bunked," Carnegie Corporation of New York, September 27, 2021, https://www.carnegie.org/our-work/article/15-myths-about-immigration-debunked/.

37. Walter Ewing, "Your Covid-19 Vaccine Was Likely Made by an Immigrant," Immigration Impact, December 14, 2020, https://immigrationimpact.com/2020/12/14/who-made-covid19-vaccine/; Alex Nowasteh and Michelangelo Landgrave, "Immigrant Health Care Workers by Occupation and State," Cato Institute, May 13, 2020, https://www.cato.org/publications/publications/immigrant-health-care-workers-occupation-state.

38. John Gramlich and Jeffrey S. Passel, "U.S. Immigrant Population in 2023 Saw Largest Increase in More Than 20 Years," Pew Research Center, September 27, 2024, https://www.pewresearch.org/short-reads/2024/09/27/u-s-immigrant-population-in-2023-saw-largest-increase-in-more-than-20-years/; "Here's What We Know about Foreign-Born Workers, and How They Compare to the Native-Born Population," Peter G. Peterson Foundation, July 18, 2024, https://www.pgpf.org/article/the-foreign-born-labor-force-of-the-united-states/.

39. US Census Bureau, "US Population to Begin Declining."

40. Sebastian Dettmers, "The Great People Shortage Is Coming—and It's Going to Cause Global Economic Chaos," *Business Insider*, October 20, 2022, https://www.businessinsider.com/great-labor-shortage-looming-population-decline-disaster-global-economy-2022-10.

41. Ivana Johnston, "Turning Silver into Gold: Are Unretired Workers a Solution to the $8.5 Trillion Labor Shortage?," *Forbes*, March 25, 2024, https://www.forbes.com/councils/forbesagencycouncil/2024/03/25/turning-silver-into-gold-are-unretired-workers-a-solution-to-the-85-trillion-labor-shortage/.

42. "Working in Germany with the Opportunity Card," Chancenkarte Deutschland, accessed January 31, 2025, https://chancenkarte.com/en/candidates/; Tyler Cowen, "Could a $70,000 Baby Bonus Solve South Korea's Fertility Crisis?," *Bloomberg Businessweek*, May 14, 2024, https://www.bloomberg.com/opinion/articles/2024-05-15/south-korea-fertility-crisis-could-public-subsidies-solve-it; "'Womenomics' in Japan," Asia Pacific Curriculum, accessed January 31, 2025, https://asiapacificcurriculum.ca/learning-module/womenomics-japan.

43. Briar Stewart, "Russia Wants a Baby Boom, but Some Women Resist Becoming a Mother for the Motherland," CBC News, September 20, 2024, https://www.cbc.ca/news/world/russia-mothers-birth-rate-1.7327712.

44. Dasl Yoon, "Nation with Lowest Birthrate Is Rocked by Soaring Sales of Dog Strollers," *Wall Street Journal*, September 8, 2024, https://www.wsj.com/world/asia/nation-low-birthrate-childlessness-dog-strollers-south-korea-e9778517.

45. "Fertility Rate, Total (Births per Woman): All Countries and Economies," World Bank Group, 2023, https://data.worldbank.org/indicator/SP.DYN.TFRT.IN.

46. Anthony Cilluffo and Neil G. Ruiz, "World's Population Is Projected to Nearly Stop Growing by the End of the Century," Pew Research Center, June 17, 2019, https://www.pewresearch.org/short-reads/2019/06/17/worlds-population-is-projected -to-nearly-stop-growing-by-the-end-of-the-century/.

47. Ed Michaels, Helen Handfield-Jones, and Beth Axelrod, *The War for Talent* (Boston, MA: Harvard Business School Press, 2001).

48. Jim Clifton, *The Coming Jobs War* (New York: Gallup Press, 2011).

49. Vespa, Medina, and Armstrong, *Demographic Turning Points*, 1.

Chapter 3

1. Ernest O'Boyle Jr. and Herman Aguinis, "The Best and the Rest: Revisiting the Norm of Normality of Individual Performance," *Personal Psychology* 65, no. 1 (2012): 79–119.

2. Jim Clifton and Jim Harter, *Culture Shock: An Unstoppable Force Is Changing How We Work and Live* (Washington, DC: Gallup Press, 2023), 68.

3. Corey Tatel and Ben Wigert, "42% of Employee Turnover Is Preventable but Often Ignored," Gallup, July 10, 2024, https://www.gallup.com/workplace/646538 /employee-turnover-preventable-often-ignored.aspx.

4. Jim Harter, "A Great Manager's Most Important Habit," Gallup, May 30, 2023, https://news.gallup.com/businessjournal/106912/turning-around-your-turnover -problem.aspx.

5. Jim Clifton and Jim Harter, *It's the Manager: Gallup Finds the Quality of Managers and Team Leaders Is the Single Biggest Factor in Your Organization's Long-Term Success* (New York: Gallup Press, 2019).

6. Richard P. Finnegan, *HR's Greatest Challenge: Driving the C-Suite to Improve Employee Engagement and Retention* (Alexandria, VA: Society for Human Resource Management, 2015), 151. Emphasis added.

7. Patrick T. Ryan and Thomas H. Lee, "What Makes Healthcare Workers Stay in Their Jobs?," *Harvard Business Review*, March 2, 2023, https://hbr.org/2023/03/what -makes-health-care-workers-stay-in-their-jobs.

8. Richard P. Finnegan, *Rethinking Retention in Good Times and Bad Breakthrough Ideas for Keeping Your Best Workers* (Boston, MA: Nicholas Brealey Publishing, 2009).

9. Finnegan, *Rethinking Retention*, 104.

10. Paul J. Zak, "The Neuroscience of Trust," *Harvard Business Review*, January–February 2017, https://hbr.org/2017/01/the-neuroscience-of-trust.

11. Travis Bradberry and Jean Greaves, *Emotional Intelligence 2.0* (San Diego, CA: TalentSmart, 2009).

12. Bill Conerly, "The Labor Market Is Tight Despite High Unemployment," *Forbes*, February 19, 2021, https://www.forbes.com/sites/billconerly/2021/02/19/the -labor-market-is-tight-despite-high-unemployment/?sh=48ba24547924.

13. Marcus Buckingham and Curt Coffman, *First, Break All the Rules* (Washington, DC: Gallup Press, 1999).

Chapter 4

1. Shane McFeely and Ben Wigert, "This Fixable Problem Costs US Businesses $1 Trillion," Gallup, March 13, 2019, https://www.gallup.com/workplace/247391/fixable -problem-costs-businesses-trillion.aspx.

2. Ken Moon, Prashant Loyalka, Patrick Bergemann, and Joshua Cohen, "The Hidden Cost of Worker Turnover: Attributing Product Reliability to the Turnover of Factory Workers," *Management Science* 68, no. 5 (2022): 3755–3767.

3. Corey Tatel and Ben Wigert, "42% of Employee Turnover Is Preventable but Often Ignored," Gallup, July 10, 2024, https://www.gallup.com/workplace/646538 /employee-turnover-preventable-often-ignored.aspx.

4. "Global Indicator: Employee Retention & Attraction," Gallup, accessed January 31, 2025, https://www.gallup.com/workplace/355238/overwhelmed-employee-turnover -stay-conversations.aspx.

Chapter 5

1. *Super Pumped: The Battle for Uber*, episode 1, "Grow or Die," directed by Allen Coulter, aired February 27, 2022, on Showtime, https://www.primevideo.com/detail /Super-Pumped-The-Battle-for-Uber/0PFHZ5XR04A376LP99IVNSXLLY.

2. Biz Carson, "Dashcam Video Shows Uber's CEO in Heated Argument with Driver over Prices," *Business Insider*, February 28, 2017, https://www.businessinsider .com/uber-ceo-travis-kalanick-argument-driver-over-prices-video-2017-2.

3. X. Frei and Anne Morriss, "Everything Begins with Trust," *Harvard Business Review*, May–June, 2020, https://hbr.org/2020/05/begin-with-trust.

4. Paul Fiorelli, "Integrity Builds Trust: What? So What? and Now What?," Institute of Business Ethics, February 23, 2023, https://www.ibe.org.uk/resource /integrity-builds-trust-what-so-what-and-now-what-blog.html.

5. Charlotte Nickerson, "Herzberg's Two-Factor Theory of Motivation-Hygiene," *Simply Psychology*, September 28, 2023, https://www.simplypsychology.org/herzbergs -two-factor-theory.html.

6. Tonya Eckert, "Managers Impact Our Mental Health More Than Doctors, Therapists—and Same as Spouses," *Business Wire*, January 24, 2023, https://www .businesswire.com/news/home/20230124005390/en/5376295/Managers-Impact-Our -Mental-Health-More-Than-Doctors-Therapists-%e2%80%94-and-Same-as-Spouses.

7. A. J. Willingham, "What Is Maslow's Hierarchy of Needs? A Psychology Theory, Explained," CNN World, August 15, 2023, https://www.cnn.com/world/maslows -hierarchy-of-needs-explained-wellness-cec/index.html.

8. "What Is Psychological Safety?" McKinsey & Company, July 17, 2023, https://www.mckinsey.com/featured-insights/mckinsey-explainers/what-is-psychological-safety.

9. Paul J. Zak, "The Neuroscience of Trust," *Harvard Business Review*, January–February 2017, https://hbr.org/2017/01/the-neuroscience-of-trust.

10. Zak, "Neuroscience of Trust."

11. Amy Adkins, "Only 35% of U.S. Managers Are Engaged in Their Jobs," Gallup, April 2, 2015, https://www.gallup.com/workplace/236552/managers-engaged-jobs.aspx.

Chapter 6

1. Amrisha Vaish, Tobias Grossmann, and Amanda Woodward, "Not All Emotions Are Created Equal: The Negativity Bias in Social-Emotional Development," *Psychological Bulletin* 134, no. 3 (2008): 383–403.

2. Pam A. Mueller and Daniel M. Oppenheimer, "The Pen Is Mightier Than the Keyboard: Advantages of Longhand Over Laptop Note Taking," *Psychological Science* 25, no. 6 (2014): 1159–1168.

Chapter 7

1. "Great Expectations: Making Hybrid Work Work," Microsoft Work Lab, March 16, 2022, https://www.microsoft.com/en-us/worklab/work-trend-index/great-expectations-making-hybrid-work-work.

2. Lily Zheng, "What Comes After DEI?," *Harvard Business Review*, January 23, 2025, https://hbr.org/2025/01/what-comes-after-dei.

3. Vanessa Fuhrmans and Te-Ping Chen, "What's Keeping Black Workers from Moving Up the Corporate Ladder?," *Wall Street Journal*, February 21, 2021, https://www.wsj.com/articles/whats-keeping-black-workers-from-moving-up-the-corporate-ladder-11613926801.

4. Ruby K. Payne, Philip DeVol, and Terie Dreussi-Smith, *Bridges Out of Poverty: Strategies for Professionals and Communities* (Highlands, TX: aha! Process inc., 2001): 11. Emphasis added.

5. Payne, DeVol, and Dreussi-Smith, *Bridges Out of Poverty*, 25.

Chapter 8

1. Kelly Main, "A Recent Survey Revealed That Hiring Managers Have a Dirty Little Secret That Is Driving High Turnover," *INC*, October 23, 2023, https://www.inc.com/kelly-main/a-recent-survey-revealed-that-hiring-managers-have-a-dirty-little-secret-that-is-driving-high-turnover.html.

2. Meta Brown, Elizabeth Setren, and Giorgio Topa, *Do Informal Referrals Lead to Better Matches? Evidence from a Firm's Employee Referral System*, Federal Reserve Bank of New York Staff Report No. 568, August 2012, https://www.newyorkfed.org/research/staff_reports/sr568.html.

3. PayrollOrg, "Survey Reveals Majority of Americans Still Living Paycheck to Paycheck," press release, PR Newswire, September 25, 2024, https://www.prnewswire.com/news-releases/survey-reveals-majority-of-americans-still-living-paycheck-to-paycheck-302257819.html.

Chapter 9

1. Ryan Pendell, "Employee Engagement Strategies: Fixing the World's $8.8 Trillion Problem," Gallup, September 11, 2023, https://www.gallup.com/workplace/393497/world-trillion-workplace-problem.aspx.

2. David Zinger, "William Kahn: Q&A with the Founding Father of Engagement," Cornerstone, December 10, 2024, https://www.cornerstoneondemand.com/resources/article/william-kahn-qa-founding-father-engagement/.

3. These data have been updated each year based on Gallup's annual reports, published on their website. The most recent data were sourced from Jim Harter, "In New Workplace, U.S. Employee Engagement Stagnates," Gallup, January 23, 2024, https://www.gallup.com/workplace/608675/new-workplace-employee-engagement-stagnates.aspx.

4. Jim Harter, "U.S. Engagement Hits 11-Year Low," April 10, 2024, Gallup, https://www.gallup.com/workplace/643286/engagement-hits-11-year-low.aspx.

5. Harter, "In New Workplace."

6. Jim Clifton and Jim Harter, *It's The Manager: Moving from Boss to Coach* (New York: Gallup Press, 2019).

7. John Sullivan, "Top Performers Produce 4x More Output and Higher Quality Referrals," *ERE*, May 6, 2013, https://www.ere.net/articles/top-performers-produce-4x-more-output-and-higher-quality-referrals.

8. Diane Doran, Amy Sanchez McCutcheon, Martin G. Evans, Kathleen MacMillan, Linda McGillis Hall, Dorothy Pringle, Susan Smith, and Antoino Valente, *Impact of the Manager's Span of Control on Leadership and Performance* (Ottawa, Ontario: Canadian Health Services Research Foundation, 2004); cited in "Span of Control: Everything You Need to Know," Human Capital Hub, October 8, 2024, https://www.thehumancapitalhub.com/articles/Span-Of-Control-Everything-You-Need-To-Know.

9. "NCSBN Research Projects Significant Nursing Workforce Shortages and Crisis," NCSBN, April 13, 2023, https://www.ncsbn.org/news/ncsbn-research-projects-significant-nursing-workforce-shortages-and-crisis.

Chapter 10

1. Jim Clifton and Jim Harter, *Culture Shock: An Unstoppable Force Is Changing How We Work and Live* (Washington, DC: Gallup Press, 2023).

2. "Pay Gains Slowed in December," ADP Pay Insights, December 2024, https://workforcereport.adp.com/.

3. Donald Sull, Charles Sull, and Ben Zweig, "Toxic Culture Is Driving the Great Resignation," *MIT Sloan Management Review*, February 21, 2023, https://sloanreview.mit.edu/article/toxic-culture-is-driving-the-great-resignation/.

4. Clifton and Harter, *Culture Shock*.

5. Chris Westfall, "Why Some Workers Would Take a 20% Pay Cut to Work from Home," February 10, 2025, https://www.forbes.com/sites/chriswestfall/2025/02/10/why-some-workers-would-take-a-20-pay-cut-to-work-from-home/.

6. Katharine Brooks, "Job, Career, Calling: Key to Happiness and Meaning at Work?," *Psychology Today*, June 29, 2012, https://www.psychologytoday.com/us/blog/career-transitions/201206/job-career-calling-key-happiness-and-meaning-work.

7. Mike Rose, *The Mind at Work: Valuing the Intelligence of the American Worker* (New York: Penguin Books, 2004), 33.

8. Barry Schwartz, *Why We Work* (New York: Simon and Schuster, TED Books, 2015), 18.

Closing Thoughts

1. "The 8 Types of Company Culture," video, 4:50, *Harvard Business Review*, December 18, 2017, https://hbr.org/video/5686668254001/the-8-types-of-company-culture.

2. Randall J. Beck and Jim Harter, "Why Great Managers Are So Rare," Gallup, https://www.gallup.com/workplace/231593/why-great-managers-rare.aspx.

3. Jim Harter and Amy Adkins, "Employees Want a Lot More from Their Managers," Gallup, April 8, 2015, https://www.gallup.com/workplace/236570/employees-lot-managers.aspx.

4. "What Is Organizational Culture? And Why Does It Matter?," Gallup, https://www.gallup.com/workplace/327371/how-to-build-better-company-culture.aspx.

5. Dale Stafford and Laura Miles, "Integrating Cultures after a Merger," December 2013, Bain & Company, https://www.bain.com/insights/integrating-cultures-after-a-merger/.

6. Clayton M. Christensen, Richard Alton, Curtis Rising, and Andrew Waldeck, "The Big Idea: The New M&A Playbook," *Harvard Business Review*, March 2011, https://hbr.org/2011/03/the-big-idea-the-new-ma-playbook.

7. Stephen Conmy, "What Does Culture Eats Strategy for Breakfast Mean?," Corporate Governance Institute, accessed January 31, 2025, https://www.thecorporategovernanceinstitute.com/insights/lexicon/what-does-culture-eats-strategy-for-breakfast-mean/.

Contact Us at C-Suite Analytics!

Our clients have reduced employee turnover by an average of 34 percent, and we help them by applying the Finnegan's Arrow model within their organizations as detailed in this book.

We work with companies large and small and provide our solution virtually or in-person at your location. We work first with executive teams by guiding them to place dollar costs on turnover and establishing retention goals for their leaders. Then we train those leaders to facilitate Stay Interviews and forecast how long each employee will stay, followed by tracking and accountability to ensure each leader achieves their retention goals and develops accurate retention forecasts.

The result for your organization is that turnover decreases, as does your number of open jobs, leading to increased productivity for your operations team along with improved employee engagement.

So if you are serious about improving turnover or engagement, please contact me at DFinnegan@C-SuiteAnalytics.com.

About the Author

Richard P. Finnegan is the global turnover expert, having cut turnover by 30 percent and more for healthcare, manufacturing, logistics, distribution centers, call centers, and other industries. He has worked globally across all inhabited continents to reduce turnover, including in Siberia, China, African gold mines, and for the CIA.

Bloomberg Businessweek magazine has said "Finnegan offers fresh thinking for solving the turnover problem in any economy." He has been similarly cited by *Forbes*, *Chief Executive* magazine, and *Consulting Magazine*. He has authored five previous books on employee retention and engagement, and his weekly *Targeting Turnover* blog contains timely recommendations on turnover fixes.

As a supremely rated speaker, Finnegan opens executives' eyes to turnover's mega-impact on their productivity and profits. He then provides strongly researched and business-driven ways to fix turnover, comparing those same solutions to the ways organizations improve sales and service.

He holds a bachelor's and graduate degrees from the Pennsylvania State University and lives in Orlando, Florida. He can be reached at DFinnegan@C-SuiteAnalytics.com or found on LinkedIn at linkedin.com/in/dick-finnegan-a718746/.

Berrett–Koehler
Publishers

Berrett-Koehler is an independent publisher dedicated to an ambitious mission: *Connecting people and ideas to create a world that works for all.*

Our publications span many formats, including print, digital, audio, and video. We also offer online resources, training, and gatherings. And we will continue expanding our products and services to advance our mission.

We believe that the solutions to the world's problems will come from all of us, working at all levels: in our society, in our organizations, and in our own lives. Our publications and resources offer pathways to creating a more just, equitable, and sustainable society. They help people make their organizations more humane, democratic, diverse, and effective (and we don't think there's any contradiction there). And they guide people in creating positive change in their own lives and aligning their personal practices with their aspirations for a better world.

And we strive to practice what we preach through what we call "The BK Way." At the core of this approach is *stewardship,* a deep sense of responsibility to administer the company for the benefit of all of our stakeholder groups, including authors, customers, employees, investors, service providers, sales partners, and the communities and environment around us. Everything we do is built around stewardship and our other core values of *quality, partnership, inclusion,* and *sustainability.*

We are grateful to our readers, authors, and other friends who are supporting our mission. We ask you to share with us examples of how BK publications and resources are making a difference in your lives, organizations, and communities at bkconnection.com/impact.

Dear reader,

Thank you for picking up this book and welcome to the worldwide BK community! You're joining a special group of people who have come together to create positive change in their lives, organizations, and communities.

What's BK all about?

Our mission is to connect people and ideas to create a world that works for all.

Why? Our communities, organizations, and lives get bogged down by old paradigms of self-interest, exclusion, hierarchy, and privilege. But we believe that can change. That's why we seek the leading experts on these challenges—and share their actionable ideas with you.

A welcome gift

To help you get started, we'd like to offer you a **free copy** of one of our bestselling ebooks:

bkconnection.com/welcome

When you claim your **free ebook**, you'll also be subscribed to our blog.

Our freshest insights

Access the best new tools and ideas for leaders at all levels on our blog at ideas.bkconnection.com.

Sincerely,

Your friends at Berrett-Koehler

MIX
Paper | Supporting
responsible forestry
FSC® C005010